PRA

M000306530

"Our leading theologian does
thinker, professor, public intellectual, and social activist—has confronted
one of the most fraught topics in American history and illuminated it with
visceral power. An enthralling, moving, and emotional journey of encounter, suffering, and victory."

—William C. McDonald, professor, University of Virginia

"*N* is an elegant, heartfelt rumination on America's crucible of race. Engaging, beautifully crafted, and analytically powerful, it masterfully employs
Twain's Huck Finn as both a literal and a figurative representation of the
nation's never-ending racial drama. By blending the narrative voice of
a memoirist and the sharp insights of a true scholar, Harris achieves a
remarkable literary triumph."

—Tim Wise, author of *White like Me: Reflections
on Race from a Privileged Son*

"James Henry Harris offers an outstanding analysis of the pain and degradation caused by using the N-word. He writes this book as a compelling story,
incorporating personal experience, historical facts, and literary criticism
that will stir your emotions, challenge your thinking, and keep you reading."

—Jacqueline Madison-McCreary, pastor, First Baptist
Church of New Market, Piscataway, New Jersey

"Harris has written a courageous memoir that confronts the long debate
over Mark Twain, *The Adventures of Huckleberry Finn*, and the use of the
N-word. Marshaling critics from Hegel to bell hooks, and calling on a family history of resistance, Harris challenges his instructor and classmates,
and in turn inspires his readers, to redress the long history of American
racism and white supremacy bound up with the epithet."

—Mark A. Sanders, professor of English and Africana
studies, University of Notre Dame

"James Henry Harris masterfully takes the reader on an experiential journey with an American classic as both analysis and memoir. *N: My Encounter with Racism and the Forbidden Word in an American Classic* articulates
the gravitas and visceral effects of the singular word in the English language, a word that still holds America in the grips of its nebulous struggle
to traverse its path of liberty and justice for all. As Harris speaks from the
heart, the reader will be forever transformed by his impassioned words."

—Lisa Baldwin-Wilson, DMin student, Samuel De Witt Proctor
School of Theology at Virginia Union University

"Incendiary in the cleanliness of its outrage, *N* by James Henry Harris gives the real-life account of a Black man blindsided by the most insufferable word in the American lexicon, and his attempt to symbolize the ensuing trauma of being ambushed by it in the halls of academia. In this pursuit, Harris offers a winning critique of race and place, with the grace of an aging scholar trying to make sense of the forbidden word."

—Tony Baugh, author of *Groan in the Throat Vol. 1: "White Supremacy Is a Religion" and Other Essays on Being Black, Keeping the Faith, and Surviving America*

"How do we resist a sign of evil without promulgating it? Mark Twain saturated and satirized the racist word; hip-hop tries to appropriate and 'flip' it. They both risk making it more pervasive and global. James Harris's way is to locate the word's cruelty in a memoir of childhood, education, and ministry—and of surviving a graduate seminar on *Huckleberry Finn*. The forbidden word is out there, as hostile as ever. His gripping, startling narratives show how and why."

—Larry D. Bouchard, University of Virginia

"Harris combines the passion and power of personal experience with a masterful display of historical and literary criticism, and the finished product is a book that goes beyond Twain's painfully derogatory stereotypes, racial epithets, and persistent myths to expose race as the enduring and central dilemma of the American experience. In compelling terms, Harris helps us understand why our claims of a post-racial society remain open to serious question and debate."

—Lewis V. Baldwin, emeritus professor of religious studies, Vanderbilt University

"In *N*, James Henry Harris presents a striking account of the psychic dislocation and spiritual pain caused by the forbidden word—encountered here in the absurd racism of Mark Twain's Pap Finn and as a tool that continues to express and enforce systemic inequity throughout American culture. Interwoven in this examination is Harris's profound testament to his family as a crucible for identity and a source of comfort and strength in the face of injustice. This is a moving and important work."

—Andrew Blossom, College of William & Mary

n

My Encounter with RACISM and the
FORBIDDEN WORD in an American Classic

James Henry Harris

FORTRESS PRESS
MINNEAPOLIS

N
My Encounter with Racism and the Forbidden Word in an American Classic

This edition is adapted from *The Forbidden Word: The Symbol and Sign of Evil in American Literature, History, and Culture* copyright © 2012 James Henry Harris and published by Cascade Books.

Scripture quotations marked (NRSV) are from the New Revised Standard Version Bible, copyright © 1989 National Council of the Churches of Christ in the United States of America. Used by permission. All rights reserved worldwide.

Scripture quotations marked (KJV) are from the King James Version.

Cover design: John M. Lucas
Cover image: From Les Aventures de Huck Finn, illustrations Achille Sirouy, 1886. Wikimedia Commons.

Print ISBN: 978-1-5064-7916-3
eBook ISBN: 978-1-5064-7917-0

Deliver us from evil.

—Matthew 6:13b (KJV)

They shouted back, "Crucify him!" Pilate asked them, "Why, what evil has he done?" But they shouted all the more, "Crucify him!"

—Mark 15:13–14 (NRSV)

They are skilled in doing evil, but do not know how to do good.

—Jeremiah 4:22c (NRSV)

And if a soul sin, and commit any of these things which are forbidden to be done by the commandments of the Lord.

—Leviticus 5:17a (KJV)

Contents

Preface

Oh no, Nig . . . nothing like that with me. I know you're no nigger, so it's alright. You can get as black as you please as far as I'm concerned since I know you're no nigger. I draw the line at that. No niggers in my family. Never have been and never will be.

—Nella Larsen, *Passing*, 1929

You can only be destroyed by believing that you really are what the white world calls a nigger. I tell you this because I love you, and please don't ever forget it.

—James Baldwin, *The Fire Next Time*, 1962

Some days, I am paralyzed by fear. And on other days, I tremble with anger about the pandemic of racism and white supremacy. But every morning when the sun rises, I live in the hope of a new day when Black people will be treated like human beings—a day when I can stop crying. As I look in the mirror and examine the furrows in my brow and the face of the man that I am—a tough and compassionate dark-brown complexioned and Black specimen of God's creation—I think to myself that nobody can tell me I am a *nigger*. Not the rappers and hip-hop artists, not the racist politicians, philosophers, theologians, historians, movie makers, scholars. Not the songwriters and poets. Not the white Capitol police, the congressional Democrats, Republicans, and white supremacists. No, nobody has the right to do that, and Mark Twain is no exception. I alone have the right to say and to know who I am. When I look in my eyes, they stare back at me in love and compassion and sorrow, reflecting the spirit of strength and weakness burdened by balancing love and hope with fear, anger, and despair. I say to myself, *James, you are a strong Black man who provides for your family and is determined to help people—all types of people, but mainly Blacks, to take pride in their Blackness.* This is the everyday lesson I drive home to my sons, Corey and Cameron, and to my community, my church, and my students.

Excellence is what I teach and what I try to model. This is not easy because in education and in community life, indifference and mediocrity are often the order of the day. Too often we expect students, coworkers, and our leaders to be marginal—to think narrowly, uncritically, and to perform minimally. I bear the pain and scars of having been threatened, criticized, and shunned by some faculty, church members, administrators, and students because I insist on excellence and Black love in and out of the classroom. I know the pain of internal exile. Because I love my people so much, I have always wanted to become a general scholar and a practical leader in Black folks' lives. This has led me to continue my education long after earning my PhD degree. I felt driven to study African American cultural life, literature, writing, and rhetoric, so I enrolled in several doctoral, MA, and MFA seminars in English literature, African American religious history and literature, short story writing, and literary criticism. I aced all of these courses, including the Mark Twain seminar on the *Adventures of Huckleberry Finn*, where I was bombarded with and burdened by the word *nigger*.

Historically, the word *nigger* was invented and embedded in white America's language and practice as a racial epithet designed to degrade and destroy the Black mind and body. It was not only a denial of respect but an intentional and systemic use of a derogatory term to infuse Black consciousness with the notion of "nothingness"—an ontological denial of being. But it did not work, because Blacks always had common sense enough to know and believe that they could not and would not be defined by their oppressor. It's in their DNA. This systematic oppression and denial of Black life from the Middle Passage to the recent murders of George Floyd and Breonna Taylor reflects four centuries of white supremacist ideology and practice throughout government, business, politics, education, and white church life. Almost every white American adult, their progenitors, and their children learned to use the word *nigger* with impunity at one time or another because it has been passed on from one generation to the next. I know this because as a child, around six or seven years old, I was first called *nigger* by a group of white children as my cousin and I walked to the corner store, Sadler's, in Matoaca, Virginia. In order to get from our house to the store, we had to walk a mile on a narrow country road, up a hill, and past a clump of poor whites who taunted us with verbal abuse propped up and sustained by the word *nigger*. That's what I remember. That's all I remember.

Now, fast-forward to January 6, 2021, during the Trump-orchestrated incitement of the mob to attack the US Capitol. The Black police officers were constantly attacked as they sought to protect the men and women of Congress from "domestic terrorists" who shouted "Hang Mike Pence!" and "Fuck Nancy Pelosi!" on camera, in plain sight of every American and people around the world. What we didn't see and hear is what the Black police officers had to endure from whites who were leaders and members of various white supremacist groups. As one account reports, "'I got called a nigger 15 times today,' [a] veteran officer shouted in the Rotunda to no one in particular.

'Trump did this and we got all of these fucking people in our department that voted for him.'"*

Think of it. Black Capitol police officers risked their lives to protect many who do everything in their power to enact laws that deny equal justice and rights to Blacks. And more, they were threatened, taunted, disrespected, and degraded by the white rioters whom the president of the United States emboldened; and by logical deduction, he gave them license to call Black police officers with guns and weapons *niggers* to their face in 2021. This is amazing and infuriating because the white folk who participated in the insurrection felt no semblance of fear in the presence of Black police officers, yet racist officers within that same force—who participated in the Capitol insurrection at the public and obvious urging of the president—continue to murder innocent, weaponless Black men and women using everyday lies such as "I felt threatened for my life" or "He was reaching for a gun." That's the real reason why the entire federal government law enforcement apparatus was passive and complicit. How could they feel threatened by their own white American president and his supporters?

The murders of Trayvon Martin, Sandra Bland, Daniel Prude, Ahmaud Arbery, Breonna Taylor, George Floyd, and many others demand that we shout from the rooftops that Black lives matter. Washington, DC, and the US Capitol represent a tale of two cities where Black protestors for justice get arrested en masse, and white supremacist protestors get to take selfies with the police and repeatedly call Black Capitol police *niggers*. And nothing is done about it because even with guns and badges, Black folk continue to stand in fear of America's modern-day

---

* See Emmanuel Felton, "Black Police Officers Describe the Racist Attacks They Faced as They Protected the Capitol," BuzzFeed News, January 9, 2021, https://www.buzzfeednews.com/article/emmanuelfelton/black-capitol-police-racism-mob.

slave masters—Donald Trump and his white supremacists all across the nation, the Congress, the hamlets, and suburbs from Virginia to California. These are the architects and sustainers of lies, propaganda, and race-hatred politics who claimed that the 2020 presidential election was stolen in Black urban areas like Philadelphia, Detroit, and Atlanta, where Trump lost. This is an insidious and nefarious race-based lie that was supported by the Republican Party. This is an American tragedy in search of a new Jim Crow—maybe a new slaveocracy.

This is not rocket science. This is the nature of racism and white supremacy. The world knows that if Blacks had stormed the Capitol, there would have been a massacre of epic proportions and scores of Black folk would have died, and the US Congress would have wasted no time in finding the leader guilty of treason, inciting a riot, murder, sedition, and so on. And that Black person would have been hanged and vilified as was Nat Turner, who was executed in Virginia on November 11, 1831.

Now I speak on the matter of the use of *nigger*, or "the N-word"—its new, more postmodern, and acceptable form. Both terms are the creations of racist white supremacy. White folk created *nigger* and now the N-word as pushback to their vile, racist epithet. But don't get it twisted; the meaning is the same. It's a tautology. *Nigger* equals the N-word, and the N-word means *nigger*, and everybody knows it. This is a play on words—a semantic and rhetorical fallacy to deceive our society into thinking something else. No, let's face it: Black people are not duped by either term, and whites have not changed their inner spirit by changing their language from Mark Twain's usage of *nigger* in *Adventures of Huckleberry Finn* to the N-word, preferred in public discourse now by white and Black intellectuals, scholars, and academics.

This is where synchronic and diachronic analysis merge. In other words, from a linguistic perspective, a diachronic analysis of the word *nigger* yields its present synchronic form, the N-word. *Nigger* is the new N-word, and the N-word is the old *nigger*. Except, on January 6, 2021, the Black Capitol police officers who were holding back the cavalry of white supremacists were called *nigger* over and over again, their uniforms and guns be damned. They were called *niggers* in spite of the preference of the literati.

Saying the N-word is deemed to be polite and acceptable, but it is deceptive and duplicitous, just like America. It is now the American word for *nigger*, except that this message has not trickled down to the racist white supremacists.

I am now some years removed from that awful experience in the class where the use of the word *nigger* was embedded on almost every page of Mark Twain's classic *Adventures of Huckleberry Finn*. There was no way for me to prevent myself from hearing the word. It was like daylight in the morning and darkness at midnight. It was omnipresent. I ask myself over and over about my own motivation to include this particular class in my educational quest to learn more about American studies, African American literature, race, religion, psychology, and social thought. To this day, I do not fully know the psychology and philosophy that drove me to learn about how this dreadful pejorative word *nigger* is applied exclusively to Black people in America. Mark Twain grew up in a white slaveholding society in which the everyday tormenting use of the word by whites of all social, economic, and political persuasions was ubiquitous. And the word persists today as hate speech by whites.

This book is about my experience of reading and encountering Twain's classic book, *Adventures of Huckleberry Finn*, for the first time as a fifty-three-year-old Black man. It is also about my feelings, flashbacks of trauma, and terror spawned by the verbalization of the word *nigger* by whites in a classroom setting where I was the only Black male, the only Black person, and the only minority.

This was indeed a class that would last a lifetime. I was already pretty rattled and unsettled because the weight of history and Black consciousness was beating me to a pulp. It's a miracle that I hadn't lost my mind from thinking about all the mean and evil things folk had said and done to me over those fifty-something years, and yet Mark Twain made me angry and sad all over again. This book is a short descant on my tangled feelings about reading the forbidden word and hearing it as a verbal assault on me and all Black people every single day. I ask myself, How can I stay sane and sober when every day brings pelting rain and gale force winds pummeling me to the ground? I get up every day because I love to see the sunrise and to feel its rays that drive the rain, the tears, away.

We drank from the river of silence. The Mississippi is a metaphor for the power of escaping the destruction of slavery and the unending quest for freedom in Twain's novel. It symbolizes racism and injustice in America; it is a cultural trope in American life. Not only that. I can also imagine the number of bodies and bones of Black lives buried at the bottom of the mighty Mississippi River.

The graduate class made an assumption: the forbidden word could be said in my presence because it could be attributed to Huck, Jim, Aunt Sally, or Pap. Racism 101. Twain himself was always protected by the professor and the rest of the students. White privilege. Nothing negative could be attributed to Twain. As far as the professor and the white students were concerned, Mark Twain was a god. And yet, I felt differently. I was not duped. In my mind, I placed Twain in the pantheon of Americans who, in one way or another, have sustained and emblazoned the word *nigger* into America's consciousness. In other words, the spirit of America—as evidenced by white supremacy proponents—has been expressed in her use of the word *nigger*, and nobody used the vile word as pejoratively and ubiquitously as America's favorite writer, Mark Twain. And he doesn't use it "the same way we does," says James Henry Harris; my sons, Cameron and Corey; the rappers and hip-hop artists; and all the Black folk I know.

James Henry Harris
Richmond, Virginia
February 2021

Chapter 1

Nothing surprises me anymore. So, I am not surprised by American racism. It's in the water and in the soil. It is long and wide and flows as freely as the Mississippi River. For the first time in my life, at age fifty-three, I'm reading Mark Twain's *Adventures of Huckleberry Finn*. Imagine me sitting alone in the classroom on the first day, a good ten minutes early. This in itself is really out of character for me because I am usually a few minutes late for everything except Sunday morning worship or a funeral. And, even these holy rituals have not completely escaped my tardiness. I am not the best example. But, on this day I wanted to counterbalance this myth—to dispel the notion that Black people are so consistently late that they have a time-consciousness of their own.

I smiled, choosing a table and a chair where I can see the door. I have a phobia about having my back to the door. I always sit where I can see how to escape. On this particular day, I also wanted to see the young graduate students who would be studying with me as they walked in. I didn't have to wait very long. The first one came strutting through the door about two minutes after I did. He was a short white male who looked to be about twenty-five years old, with shaggy hair and rimmed glasses that made him appear a bit older. I noticed a strange-looking tattoo on both of his arms. His arms were long and his hands were big—like those of the boxer Oscar De La Hoya. I guess I noticed this because his hands and arms were disproportionate to his rather diminutive body. I didn't want him to see me gazing, so I waited until he reached over in his backpack before I ventured another glance. The right arm had a tattoo of what appeared to be a flag on it. I leaned forward slowly to get a better look. Then, like a thief, I turned and looked out the window. I thought to myself, *Is that the American flag or a Confederate flag?* In Richmond, the Confederacy is kept alive by statues on Monument Avenue, which are slowly being removed after the protests of 2020. Still, it is lined with statues of soldiers who fought for the South during the Civil War. I was just about to ask the meaning of his body art when a group of young students came through the door and rescued me.

There were about seven or eight of them, but they made so much noise I thought it was more than the room could hold. After a minute or so, a young white girl barely in her twenties walked in. She had spiked hair and carried a purple pocketbook. She looked like a member of a rock band. Next came an older woman with a leather briefcase. She looked like a teacher in her late forties. I later learned that she was a lawyer who drove fifty miles down to Richmond from Williamsburg just to take this one class on *Adventures of Huckleberry Finn.*

By the time the clock struck four, there were ten people sitting around four tables pushed together for the once-a-week seminar held every Thursday from 4:00 to 6:40 p.m. The professor must have come in shielded by the noise and a number of students who had descended upon the classroom just a minute or so before the seminar was scheduled to begin. He was directly under what looked to me like a portrait of Robert E. Lee, the Confederate general. Or maybe it could have been Lee's partner, Stonewall Jackson. They all look alike to me. It's the horses they ride and the uniforms they wear. The room was, in fact, an old dining room converted into a classroom in a building that was an antebellum plantation mansion. In my mind's eye, the room became a mirror of old sins and transgressions.

It began to speak of the past. I could see the slave master and his wife ordering breakfast and telling the Black servants that the floors needed to be swept and cleaned, and the pots and pans scrubbed, and the silver platters polished at least an hour before sunset. The images overwhelmed me. My mind became a matrix of past and present, and even the future was bearing down on me, causing me to tremble in my seat.

I thought about how this was the sort of place where privilege and patriarchy were born and raised, nurtured by the tradition of Black folk cooking and serving delectables on shining silver platters to their slave master's delight. This is where Black folk learned the ways of white folk. This is where Black folk acquired the necessary astuteness to speak, breathe, and exist without the Otherness that defined them. They learned how to pretend that everything in life was fine and dandy when life itself was a pride-swallowing siege. It is where the practices of smiling, "soft-shoeing," and "cooning" were refined into a tradition of degradation and self-deprecation. This is the house in which Blacks learned to wear masks and store their anger in their hearts and souls until it could be unleashed like hellfire and brimstone.

My sitting in this classroom seemed a tad incredible, considering that a little more than 150 years earlier, I would have been forced to help build the walls that now surrounded me. As I looked at these walls, they returned my stare, and my imagination was seized by the history that had brought these walls to be. These walls spoke of that history. Even the layers upon layers of paint and lacquer could not conceal their speech. They spoke a language that only I could hear. I could feel it. I could understand it, though I couldn't speak it. They spoke of my ancestors with callused hands and bent backs, building these walls day and night. In the heat and in the cold, in the rain and in the sunshine. I could also see them big and Black, bent over with callused hands, scrubbing the windows that made the sun-drenched carpet look like a fading rainbow. I could hear the horrors trapped within these plastered walls—the muted screams of Black women and girls being raped by their slave masters, the moans and groans of field hands being whipped by overseers. I could hear the cries of families torn apart in the name of profit—sold on the auction block for a few pieces of silver. The acrid smell of human bodies, burnt and branded by the slave master's whip and the sun's heat, filled my senses. I had a total eclipse of the brain as sorrow and anger seeped through my spirit.

Everybody was still buzzing about themselves, but I was lost in deep thought about the "Middle Passage," or the forced voyage of enslaved Africans across the Atlantic Ocean to the shores of America. I thought of words like *commodity, nihilism, slavocracy,* and the banality of evil. Though I sat frozen in a trance, my imagination was set ablaze and fueled by the agonizing winds of history. Had I been listening, I would have known what the other class members had said as they introduced themselves. But I was beside myself, I was overwhelmed by the agony of my slave ancestors. I tried to remember my African dialect—my native language. I know this sounds unreal to a person whose language is his own, but my language is not mine. I strain in my dreams and my imagination to remember, but I can't.

What should I say about myself? The class was waiting. They were all staring at me. I was thinking. I was teetering on the brink of—delirium. Anticipation lurked in the furrows and freckles of a sea of white faces. Suddenly, I realized that I was the only African American in the class.

Ten or twelve students stared at me, puzzled and confused, but I couldn't respond. Ernest Gaines's opening line from *A Lesson before Dying* came back to me: "I WAS NOT THERE, yet I was there."* That was my condition. I was in a twilight

---

* Ernest J. Gaines, *A Lesson before Dying* (New York: Vintage, 1993), 3.

zone that was my own purgatory. I felt trapped between past and present. I thought I heard some mumbling or a snicker or two, but I couldn't snap out of it. I started thinking . . . why weren't more Blacks in this class? At least one other Black person—just one so I wouldn't feel so isolated, so alone. Could this really be so, that only one Black male and no Black females had registered for this class on Mark Twain? Did they know something that I didn't know? Was Mark Twain considered a racist? Or was Huck Black, as Shelley Fisher Fishkin had asked? Was he really that different from all other white Americans? There was so much that I didn't know about Mark Twain and so much that I didn't know about myself. My feelings took hold of me and I was surprised not by the joy of C. S. Lewis, but by pain and anger. Even a sorrowful sadness blanketed my face.

Why? In a university with thirty thousand students, how could this absence of Black students be explained? Maybe studying English literature in an age of technology was just too impractical for most young Black people. Maybe there was too much reading and writing and analysis and not enough sound bites. This class was not postmodern enough. It was not in the business school or the school of education. Maybe reading *Adventures of Huckleberry Finn* was just too painful. Maybe they really did know that the class conjured too many emotions and caused too much stress. Or maybe other Blacks just couldn't see how this class would help them get a job to pay the rent and buy the groceries. It was too esoteric and not pragmatic enough. I already had a job. Two jobs!

I admit it is hard to survive in the jungles of our cities and communities. It is hard to read and study the life and words of old white men like Mark Twain and his progenitors—Plato, Aristotle, and the Greek tragedians Aeschylus, Euripides, and others—when energy prices are sky high and the cost of a loaf of bread and a pound of anything edible is almost prohibitive. It could be a pound of cheese or a pound of bologna. This is a common folks' food—like sardines and saltine crackers. Poor folks' delectables. These are the realities that most Black people face. This is the world where some people were treated differently because of their dark skin and their dual African and American connection—like Sojourner Truth, Harriet Tubman, Nat Turner, or Frederick Douglass. Like me and a million others. It seems that the axis through American slavery makes the difference in life. We had a WASP neighbor a few years ago whose children were patients of a Black pediatrician who was a medium-brown-complexioned person with straight hair. The skin color was more Black than anything else. I knew the doctor to be African American, but my neighbor, in discussing her children's physician, indicated that their doctor was Indian or Lebanese. I was not about to burst her bubble and tell her that her children's doctor was in fact Black. It was okay for him to be anything except African American. The texture of his hair helped them to ignore the tone and color of his skin. Maybe that's why some Black folk are hair freaks—obsessed with perms, wigs, extensions, weaves, relaxers. The goal is to transform kinky hair into straight hair, which is said to be "good hair." When a Black woman has long, flowing, straight hair, other Blacks will quickly say, "Child, that's not her hair. She bought that hair from the Koreans. Can't you tell where her real, God-given hair ends?" Your skin can be as Black as soot, but if your hair is straight like the Asians and not kinky, then white folks will call you Indian or Asian or Hawaiian, but not Black or African American.

I thought my reasoning about hair was simply cultural until I read Philip Roth's Pulitzer Prize–winning novel *American Pastoral*, in which he describes the main character's wife, Dawn Levov, Miss New Jersey's efforts to become Miss America. The narrator goes on and on about the details and intricacies of the pageant and then he interjects, "The Southern girls in particular, Dawn told him, could really lay it on: 'Oh, you're just so wonderful, your hair's so wonderful . . .'" Then the narrator utters these words: "The veneration of hair took some getting used to for a girl as down-to-earth as Dawn; you might almost think, from listening to the conversation among the other girls, that life's possibilities resided in hair—not in the hands of your destiny but in the hands of your hair."

The veneration of hair is not simply a fetish for Black people. And, it was not the veneration of hair in the first place. It was the value and importance of hair texture. Straight versus kinky. White versus Black. That's where the issue becomes more social and psychological than aesthetic. Still, I was glad to see that I wasn't the only one who had such beliefs about hair. Henry Louis Gates in *Colored People* also gives us a short dissertation about Black people and their obsession with "nappy hair on colored heads."

For Blacks, this veneration of straight hair exemplifies the desire to be like whites and to loathe that which is Black. The long hard fight for equality and justice in public education was hair- and skin color–related.

In 1950, Black psychologists Kenneth Clark and his wife Mamie Phipps Clark published the findings of their legendary doll study, demonstrating and documenting how racial segregation impacted the self-esteem of Black children. When the Clarks asked little Black children between three and seven years old to choose between identical Black and white dolls, the majority of Black children preferred the white doll and attributed positive characteristics to it. When asked to color a picture of themselves, the same children used white or yellow crayons. Society, in the form of segregation and racism, had taught the children to hate the color of their skin and the texture of their hair. The US Supreme Court specifically cited this study in the 1954 *Brown v. Board of Education* decision. The Clarks taught society about the effects of racial oppression on the behavior and actions of Black children in the form of their Supreme Court testimony. But this was a lesson Black folks have been learning and relearning every day of their lives before and after the Clark study.

Later, reading the course description online, I reasoned that to most young people, Mark Twain's *Adventures of Huckleberry Finn* probably seemed a waste of time. It would be much more practical to study the American pragmatists Sojourner Truth, Fannie Lou Hamer, Ella Baker, William James, Charles Peirce, Ralph Waldo Emerson, Frederick Douglass, W. E. B. Du Bois, or Booker T. Washington than to be confronted with reading and hearing the word *nigger* again and again. I had certainly heard about the book and its contents, but never thought to read it until now.

I was on sabbatical for a year, but my sabbatical was really not a time to rest because I had to wrestle with the language and meanings of Mark Twain and Joseph Conrad and Charles Chestnutt. A language laden with the forbidden word *nigger*. A Sabbath is a time of daily, weekly, monthly, or yearly rest as a result of recognizing the work that God has allowed us to do. It is a spiritual experience that suggests the beneficiary of such a deserved and well-earned gift will take time to bask in the opportunity to meditate and reflect, to write, to read, and to plan for the future—absorbing the sights and sounds of adventure and wonder. To the intellectual, this is ultimate pleasure, freedom, and serenity. The ancient rabbis taught that this *menuha* makes God's creation complete. Without rest, creation is unfinished. Jewish scholar and theologian Abraham Joshua Heschel says that the Sabbath is an atmosphere, not a date: "The Sabbath teaches all beings whom to praise." Yet my own sabbatical was hard to fully embrace. It was somewhat out of character for me; except, I reasoned, that my study of literature was indeed in praise of God. I wanted to spend time studying and learning a new discipline—conquering another subject in praise of God's gift of love and grace to me.

English literature, rhetoric, and writing had been a part of my theology and humanities training, but now I was determined to focus on literature and writing fiction and nonfiction. I am possessed by a desire to read more works by some of the Black literati: Nella Larsen, Ernest Gaines, Ralph Ellison, Langston Hughes, Charles Chestnutt, Toni Morrison, Marita Golden, Zora Neale Hurston, Richard Wright, James Baldwin, and Charles Johnson. And not just Black writers, but others such as James Joyce, Joseph Conrad, Adrienne Rich, Albert Camus, Vladimir Nabokov, and the so-called king of American literature, Mark Twain. I was excited, but I was also sorely afraid because these days education is highly technological and I am so Neanderthal. Everything is done online: application, registration, drop/add, reading assignments, grades, etc. I have been in school off and on for thirty years, long before everyone started coming to class with a laptop and a Jumpdrive. Believe it or not, I still write with a pen or a pencil and use a notebook, the old-fashioned kind made of paper with lines to write on. I was afraid that I would be out of place in a postmodern craze of self-absorption and subjectivity. The environment of laptop computers and online research was daunting. And, that was not the major fear. The weakness of my understanding of literature scared me so much that I almost decided to forgo learning anything new. I have no natural talent for this type of learning, given that I can barely ever get a story straight. The story of my own life is an infinite search for a self that is in perpetual motion.

Still, I picked up the telephone, called the university, and set up a meeting with the chairperson of the English department to discuss the fact that I had done twelve seminars of graduate work in philosophical theology, ethics, and culture at the University of Virginia in Charlottesville. I was doing that to augment my teaching ability—not seeking another degree. I was readily received by the department chair and assistant dean, an expert in American literature. She was a charming and compassionate woman who encouraged me to register for six courses. "Some credit hours can be transferred from the many graduate courses you have taken," she said. "That sounds great for a guy like me," I responded. I had accumulated straight As and A-minuses while studying at some of the Commonwealth of Virginia's best universities.

Once in a particularly engaging seminar where the discussion centered around American democracy, I interjected that Jeffersonian democracy was grounded in duplicity, inequality, and racism. I went on to say that not only did Jefferson own slaves while writing about liberty and justice for all, but he was also a slave trader and sexually active with Sally Hemings, a fourteen-year-old slave and half-sister of his deceased wife. Some historians have written that he is the father of her six children who looked a lot like him, to the amazement of neighbors and visitors to Monticello. "Is this modern-day sexual abuse?" I asked. I said that he was a promoter of the commodification of the Black body, explaining that the duplicitous behavior of Jefferson was in fact as American as Twain's use of *nigger. "Dad blame it."* Talk about democracy! All the whites in the room knew this and more. And yet there was a deafening silence, like a dark pall of smoke and ash had engulfed the entire classroom. Again, I was the only Black in the room and all eyes were jabbing my soul as if I had committed a heinous crime. Smiles turned to frowns. Puffy white faces became red as Hanover tomatoes; smooth brows became deeply furrowed, and the young white doctoral students refused to recognize that there was more than one voice in the room. I had spoken up that day after sitting in silence for a long time. I was hoping that I would not be compelled to speak. But nobody, not even the professor, seemed willing to acknowledge that there is an "otherness" that must be heard if learning is to take place. Long before that class, I realized how political and propagandizing American education really is. I also felt that younger Blacks had to be struggling with their identity as African Americans in environments that often brushed aside the Black experience. *Liberal Arts ain't too liberal after all*, I thought to myself. Univocity is the order of the day.

When my son graduated with a JD/MBA from Boston College Law School and the Carrol School of Business, thirty-five family members and friends made the trip to Newton, Massachusetts, to witness this grand event. I noticed that of the nearly three hundred graduates, only three were African American. This was one percent of the graduating class. Looking at the family and friends walking into the grand refectory together, my son said, "Dad, I have never seen this many Black people here during my four years on this campus."

"I know you're right. This is a pretty elitist school, you know. Senator and presidential candidate John Kerry and the Black congressman from Virginia, Bobby Scott, graduated from here."

"Yeah, I know, Dad."

"Look at the high ceilings and the walls paneled in California redwood or is that red oak? The Jesuits *ain't* doing too bad," I said.

I could tell he was happy because everybody could witness the pride of the Black family in his accomplishments. We all graduated from Boston College Law School and Business School that same day.

Before the commencement ceremony, we had lunch together in the law school cafeteria. It was for the graduates and their families. I told the hostess that we had a busload of people from Virginia coming in at any minute. "Can you help me hold these six tables for my family?" I pleaded.

"I'll try to keep them for you," she said while gesturing to her colleague to help her hold the tables. I went to help direct our family and friends to the right place. When I returned, all the tables were gone except one. I asked the hostess what happened, and she threw up her hands and said, "Sorry. I couldn't stop them. There are no reservations, you know." Unable to sit together, we integrated ourselves into the sea of Jews and Gentiles, Catholics and Protestants, who were there.

Throughout the day I observed and took mental notes on the state of graduate education and the conditions that Black people still have to negotiate to survive and get ahead. *Well, so much for diversity and inclusion*, I thought. Culture means acculturation to most white folk, even in the prestigious liberal universities: theology and culture, religion and culture, philosophy and culture. In my theology and culture seminar at the University of Virginia, the focus was on St. Augustine, Schleiermacher, and Kathryn Tanner. This is the extent of the worldview regarding the study of God and humankind—theology and culture's only axis was through Western Europe and the United States' kinship to Europe. Africa and the African diaspora played no part in the formal discussion of culture. For Black folk negotiating graduate school, school is a face-to-face experience of racism and exclusion.

Chapter 2

"Mr. Harris," I finally heard someone say. The class was in full swing. Everyone had introduced themselves during my mental hiatus. It turned out that the voice belonged to a tall, balding white man who taught the class. He was a Mark Twain scholar and devotee of some notoriety. He appeared to be a little annoyed at me: "We are waiting for you to introduce yourself." He mustered up a smile, and so did I.

"My apologies," I began. "My name is James Henry. I am in the graduate English literature program here." I thought I had offered enough information, but the faces of the students showed that they were not satisfied with my terse response. Some smiled with anxious excitement; others frowned with concern and anticipation. They expected me to say more, but I didn't know what more to say, and if the truth be told, I didn't want to say much about myself. Minimalism was the order of the day for me. I cleared my throat and continued: "I am just here to learn." This time I thought I had finished. The professor thanked all who shared words about who they were and what they expected from the course and asked us to open our books to one of his favorite passages.

I didn't have my copy of *Adventures of Huckleberry Finn* in front of me, as the others did; nor had I, in my introduction, talked about my expectations from the class. I reached for my briefcase that I carried as a book bag. It had fallen under the table. I didn't want to be too distracting, but when I couldn't feel the book immediately, I had to pull it from under the table, open it, and look through it. I thought I had put it in a place where I could readily grab it. Papers ruffled as I fingered through my briefcase, which I should have cleaned out but had not. The crinkled pages of my book crepitated under the weight of my short pudgy fingers. I was shocked by the loud sound. Clearly, I did not know what passage I was looking for. Finding comfort in this class was next to impossible. It was the forbidden word—*nigger*—that made white supremacy evident to me every single day. I was alone in a zone that no one else could feel. The white students appeared to be OK with the daily dose of the utterance of the word. I was normally a Zelig, but in this class, I stayed to myself, one step from the door, afraid of being lured into a fistfight by the slip of the tongue or the word that Mark Twain seemed to love more than any other. It is not the word *adventures* or *Huckleberry* that controls the book, but it is the singular word *nigger,* which is both subject and predicate, noun and verb, all at the same time. I caught the lawyer's eyes glaring at me with what I took to be annoyed frustration. And my own skepticism and gut feeling kicked into high gear. *Another barracuda from William & Mary or the University of Virginia,* I thought. A barrister, maybe. Everything about her looked slightly British to me. I could hardly wait to hear her speak. She looked like a nobby member of the British Parliament as she glided across the room with her nose in the air like Queen Elizabeth or members of the wealthy uptight Banks family in "Mary Poppins." Most of us had to leave class and go to an evening job at McDonald's, at the grocery store, or as a frontline worker at Walmart or Tyson Foods. The three teachers in the class had to go home and grade homework and scratch and scramble for a dollar because public school teachers and some Black college professors are grossly underpaid and unappreciated. This particular woman seemed to be a privileged socialite unaffected by the everyday struggles of the rest of us. But that was my perception and my interpretation. My situation and my story. My imagination on autopilot. I was making it difficult for her to hear what page number the class was being asked to turn to. I pulled my book from my briefcase and put it on the table. It was a paperback book whose cover showed bent corners, and the first few pages were permanently creased because of the way it had been stuffed into my case. The class apparently had no time to wait for me. They were already following along as the professor recited his favorite passage from the book. I was tempted to ask the young redheaded woman beside me what page we were on, but I decided that I had already been too disruptive for a few folk in the class. So I opted to simply lean forward and sneak a peek over her shoulder. They were on page thirty-three. As I turned to that page, I heard nothing the professor was saying. When I looked up at him, I saw that he was not reading but reciting this section of the book from memory. I started to listen and to squirm. I became very fidgety. I felt nervous and unsettled. I was a muggle when it came to Twain's writings but an expert on recognizing oppression. For me, Twain and *Adventures of Huckleberry Finn* is the perfect avatar for American racism and white supremacy.

I couldn't believe how I was feeling and how my mind and body were reacting to hearing the forbidden word, *nigger*, by a white man. Well, I'd thought it was forbidden. As the professor recited Huck's father Pap Finn's drunken palaver with what I interpreted to be a joyful glee, I struggled with my feelings. It had been so long since I had heard a white person verbalize the word *nigger* without hesitation. But it was right there, embedded in the text the professor chose to recite. I cannot eradicate this haunting introductory recital from my mind. The professor lifted his tall, lanky body from the chair and began to *speak from memory*. The front of the class was his stage as his presence filled the room. I felt like Mark Twain had risen from the dead as Professor Wilson burst forth in his booming mimetic voice:

Call this a govment! Why, just look at it and see what it's like. . . .

Oh yes, this is a wonderful govment, wonderful. Why, looky here. There was a free nigger there, from Ohio; a mulatter, most as white as a white man. He had the whitest shirt on you ever see, too, and the shiniest hat and there ain't a man in that town that got as fine clothes as what he had; and he had a gold watch and chain, and a silver-headed cane—the awfulest old gray-headed nabob in the state. And what do you think? They said he was a p'fessor in a college, and could talk all kinds of languages, and knowed everything. And that ain't the wust. They said he could *vote*, when he was at home. Well, that let me out. Thinks I, what is the country coming to? It was 'lection day, and I was just about to go and vote, myself, if I warn't too drunk to get there; but when they told me there was a state in this country where they'd let that nigger vote, I drawed out. I says I'll never vote agin. Thems the very words I said; they all heard me; and the country may rot for all me—I'll never vote agin as long as I live. And to see the cool way of that nigger—why he wouldn't a give me the road if I hadn't shoved him out o' the way. I says to the people, why ain't this nigger put up at auction and sold?—that's what I want to know. And what do you reckon they said? Why they said he couldn't be sold till he'd been in the State six months, and he hadn't been there that long yet. There, now—that's a specimen. They call that a govment that can't sell a free nigger till he's been in the State six months. Here's a govment that calls itself a govment, and lets on to be a govment, and thinks it is a govment, and yet's got to set stock-still for six whole months before it can take a hold of a prowling, thieving, infernal, white-shirted free nigger and—

When the professor finally finished his performance of Pap's invidious diatribe, I thought to myself how clever Mark Twain had been in capturing Pap Finn's spirit and the spirit of America toward Blacks. Even the most despicable, low-down, drunken white man could glory in his superiority to Blacks. Twain had been right about that. And not just an ordinary Black. He was not a slave, nor a farm hand. Not a janitor or jackleg preacher. Not a busboy or butler. Not even a gifted musician or a dancer. But an educated and distinguished professor. A man of letters like James Baldwin, Ralph Waldo Emerson, Michel de Montaigne, Wole Soyinka, or Henry David Thoreau. Like Johann von Goethe or Gustave Flaubert. Like Frederick Douglass or Langston Hughes. Smart and proud like Harriet Tubman, Zora Neale Hurston, W. E. B. Du Bois and Booker T. Washington. A free human being of letters. A scholar and an intellectual of high social and moral character. And yet, Huck's father, Pap, felt and displayed a condescending attitude driven by patriarchy and white privilege. Pap Finn was a worthless, scabrous scamp who possibly didn't know a noun from a verb or a subject from an object. And yet he felt that he was better than or superior to the most educated and accomplished Black intellectual. If Pap were superior to a free Black professor, then the Black man was indeed an animal. A nonbeing. A piece of wood. A *nigger*. The nerve of my professor. *The gall of him*, I thought to myself as he brought his raspy mimesis to a close. My mind was still trying to process what I was witnessing with my eyes and hearing with my own ears. The professor's unmitigated gall was decorated by a verdant coat of sincerity mixed with indifference and admiration, a posture that would persist throughout the semester. This was only the beginning. He wanted every person in the class to memorize and recite a passage from *Adventures of Huckleberry Finn* as a final course requirement. Well, blow me down. I didn't think I knew myself well enough to do it. And besides, I was too weak to satirize myself with words written by Mark Twain. On second thought, I said to myself, *What the hell*; I have ten to twelve more weeks to think about it.

Imagine my feelings. I was in the cavernous pit. No, I felt that I was caught in the infernal flames of Dante's hell. I was burning up with anxiety and anger. I felt like screaming, and yet I kept my composure. I was being torn apart because I, too, was a professor. I was acquainted with the psychology of Sigmund Freud and Carl Jung. But, I felt like my identity was being battered and blasted by the power of the words of the professor for this course, of Huck's father Pap, and Mark Twain himself. They were searing and stinging because for the first time I heard the powerful and destructive sound of them. I learned that very day the ear is more revealing than the eye: the tone, the cadence, the emphasis, the volume, the precision of language. For a moment, I could hardly breathe. I was choked by the sound. Hearing the word *nigger* was biting. Stifling. It drained my body of all energy. Reason had been cut off at the root. I needed some water, but I was afraid that water would make me vomit. I was having an allergic reaction to the sound of the word. To see the word on the page or to read it silently is not the same as hearing it recited out loud by a white man. Aloud the forbidden word was stultifying and suffocating. I could tell that the professor had spent years practicing reciting this particular pericope from the Holy Bible of English literature—*Adventures of Huckleberry Finn*. No exegesis was needed for me to interpret this event. I thought of Paul Ricoeur, the French philosopher whom I had studied. The dialectic between event and meaning was crystal clear to me now. It was painful enough to read the words on a page, but to hear them recited was more than I had bargained for. In the short paragraph that Professor Wilson would recite, the word *nigger* was used six times. *Elongated. Emphatic. Enunciated in Southern intellectual style.* Did I hear indifference and disinterest, or was it enmity and venomous hatred not muzzled by tepid respect but boldly and limpidly stated and sanctioned by the "govment"? And, I admit it's a bit irrational, but no amount of whisky could obfuscate that fact. Pap knew exactly what he was saying and whom he spoke for—even in his drunkenness. At least that's the way I felt. I was convinced. In my emotional view, the class professor, Pap, and Mark Twain himself were all complicit in the use of the forbidden word. Believe it or not, I felt as if I was being lynched in a public square. I was being castrated by the cascading sound and the mocking tone of each syllable. *Nig-ger.* And yet, I knew that Mark Twain had produced a classic and wise meditation on race here. It occurred to me that he was a contrary old nabob!

I was in a dilemma. Sitting there that first day of class, I felt that the instructor of the class was as drunk as Pap, intoxicated by the language, the screen through which he recited these verses. But it was little comfort to know that he was the paragon of sobriety. I could not separate the forbidden word from Mark Twain, Pap, or the class professor. In my mind, they were all one. They were complicit in their denigration of an educated Black man. That was me they were talking about. I too was the Black p'fessor. And yet, the speaker in the written text and the person reciting the text were not the same—or were they? If Paul Ricoeur is right in saying that "the text is mute" because the author is dead, then why was I so fraught with anger and pain upon hearing the word *nigger* over and over again? This text was not mute. It was loud, boisterous, and clear. While Twain is indeed dead, the professor of the class was not dead, and in my mind, these were also his words. He hid behind the text as I felt the searing pain and agony of each syllable every time the forbidden word was spoken. Was this fiction or not? I could not really tell. The text spoke oh so loudly—like a thunderstorm or even a Hurricane Katrina. I was the signified one.

This first class was a prelude to a semester that was full of grinding torture for me. I felt I was on trial for being a runaway slave or a falsely accused murderer. I was very race conscious. I am not exaggerating. I felt like I was "nigger Jim" or Jefferson in Ernest Gaines's novel *A Lesson before Dying*, whose defense attorney had called him a hog, an animal, a worthless inhuman being without the capacity to plan and think. That day at that hour, I could only remember hearing the one word *N-I-G-G-E-R*. Everything else was mute. How was I going to make it through a class where the forbidden word was not really forbidden but rather was seen and heard on almost every page of Mark Twain's book *Adventures of Huckleberry Finn*? More than 211 times. All negative. All used as a vile racial epithet: condescendingly, with impunity, with malice and forethought, with evil intent, banefully, casually, symbolically, and thoughtfully cynical.

I heard the forbidden word *nigger* more times than I care to remember that first day of class, January 18, 2006, just a few days after the birthday of Dr. Martin Luther King Jr. This was the real irony. I thought I was in another world, transported back in time. I thought of the Middle Passage, which is the symbol of modernity and the meaning behind America's understanding of democracy and capitalism. I thought of my ancestors who were on the slave ship bound for America—"freedom land." I thought that everybody including Mark Twain, Huck Finn, Pap Finn, Miss Watson, and the class professor were all calling me *nigger* on the sly. While the professor and the rest of the class were talking, I was having an out-of-body experience. A perpetual anamnesis. A fifty-something-year-old Black man taken back to the time when he was seven or eight years old. My mind wandered. The forbidden word brought back pungent and painful memories that I thought had been forgotten.

The seminar ended at 6:50 p.m. I had experienced trouble of the mind and the soul. But, for now, I had survived the first round. The first day. The first class.

I realized I was caught in the clutches of alienation and despair. It was largely of my own making because nobody in the room knew me before I introduced myself that day. These were all young whites who very likely didn't think of me the way I felt they did. And, they didn't think of themselves as racists or bigots. And, neither did the professor do anything blatantly wrong except recite the word *nigger* from the page. But that was more than enough to alienate me from everybody else because I was already alienated by a grim social reality. For all I knew, nobody in that room, or everybody in the room, was prejudiced or racist. It's hard to interpret the mind of the South. This was my struggle and my battle born of a tension in my inner history—a tension in my spirit and in my soul. This alienation taunted and gripped me from the moment the class began and from the moment the forbidden word was first seen on the page and read aloud. Hearing the word was more painful than seeing it. In its aurality, it harbored all the years of hate and evil that were invested in it. And, I didn't know about anyone else, but I could feel the historical weight of the word around my neck, choking my breath away. Doesn't this sound familiar?

Chapter 3

I was already angry, but by the end of the first class, I felt flayed by the sharp edges of a single word. It was like the serrated blade of a knife cutting away at my self-esteem. And, to make matters worse, we were all assigned chapters for the next class meeting. The process was simple enough. We had to count off, like children learning their numbers, starting with the person to the left of the professor. Your number was your chapter to discuss during the next few class meetings. Mine was chapter eight, or what I call "Sunrise at Jackson Island." I was eighth in a sequence that spread throughout the semester—responsible for chapters eight, sixteen, twenty-four, thirty-two, etc. We didn't get to my chapter until the third class session—three weeks into the semester. Most of the language in that chapter is so elegant and beautiful—descriptive and picturesque from the very beginning. And, yet, I am tortured by my own feelings—vacillating between love and hate from one page to another. As this chapter opens, Twain sounds like a poet and prose master:

> The sun was up so high when I waked, that I judged it was eight o'clock. I laid there in the grass and the cool shade, thinking about things and feeling rested and ruther comfortable and satisfied. . . . There was freckled places on the ground where the light sifted down through the leaves, and the freckled places swapped about a little, showing there was a little breeze up there. A couple of squirrels sat on a limb and jabbered at me very friendly.

I was captivated by the perfect picture of daybreak. I thought about the beauty of nature, how I love the fall and spring, and Twain as an environmentalist. I could see Huck lying in the woods on a bed of leaves and grass as the sunlight cascaded through the trees. But, it was the "thinking about things" in the opening lines of the chapter that sparked my own memory. This would be more evident as chapter eight began to unfold with Huck discovering that someone else was also sleeping on Jackson Island:

> By and by I was close enough to have a look, and there laid a man on the ground. It most give me the fantods. He had a blanket around his head, and his head was nearly in the fire. I set there behind a clump of bushes, in about six foot of him, and kept my eyes on him steady. It was getting gray daylight, now. Pretty soon he gapped and stretched himself, and hove off the blanket, and it was Miss Watson's Jim! I bet I was glad to see him. I says: "Hello, Jim!" and skipped out.

When I read that Jim "gapped and stretched himself," I thought of my sweet momma who always used the same language. She would say, "The baby is gapping and must be tired; he need to take a nap." That brief memory shook my consciousness and caused a momentary lapse in my thinking—a lapse that made me cry as I thought about my own dear mother. The emotion had come out of thin air. It fell upon me like a bucket of warm milk.

Like Huck, Jim had also run away. Huck wanted freedom from his father and Jim wanted freedom from slavery. He didn't want to fall into the hands of a "nigger trader" because he had overheard Miss Watson's plans to sell him down the river: "I hear ole missus tell de widder she gwyne to sell me down to Orleans, but she didn't want to, but she could git eight hund'd dollars for me." Jim was no fool. He understood the meaning of chattel slavery. It was an evil system grounded in economics and commerce. Somebody needs to pay Black people for three hundred years of free and forced labor. Maybe free college or a small house mortgage-free or free health care for all descendants of enslaved people!

I thought to myself, *This is where the book really begins.* The first seven chapters are all prologue. The situation and the story begin to merge right here in chapter eight, where Huck and Jim meet for the first time as runaways and form a pact that binds them together in the adventurous search for freedom. It was also the race issue. The nigger Jim and the white boy Huck on Jackson Island, an island that Huck had already said "I was boss of it," speaking as a typical and privileged white American male. The boss.

This was the chapter where the use of *nigger* begins its ubiquitous forays into the story. And its use caused me to think about things in my own life—especially when I, as a child, was first called a nigger. I blurted out in class that I wore the marks and scars of America's nigger, and Twain's pelting use of the word felt more like the sharp jabs of a dagger than like the drops of rain winding down on the scalp of my bald head.

"Has anyone in here ever been called *nigger*?" I asked. The answer was a thundering silence so piercing that you could hear its palpable sounds only in the deep breaths that each body began to take. I knew before asking the question that silence was the only possible answer, so I felt guilty for making such a rhetorical flourish. It was a sophistry that I had mastered and grown to love although I knew it was probably unfair and deceptive. My Black skin had, for once, given me the advantage to pose a question that not a single white person in the room could answer in the affirmative. While I took pleasure in the hovering silence, it provided no lasting consolation. This was my personal burden and my struggle, and I was not handling it too well. I had a long way to go and even further to grow, to the point of recognizing how hurt and angry I had become. It was bad for my health because high cholesterol, high blood pressure, and high blood sugar ran in my family, and at fifty-three years old, I was already becoming a victim of them all. I was really a wreck. Race had played a major role in my health, and while it was evident to me, no one else in the room had experienced the pressures of daily living in two worlds with two different consciences. Double consciousness was a state of being for me. I was a self divided. It is also the stuff that makes for some forms of depression, schizoid and paranoid behavior. And, at times, I'm a bona fide paranoid African American male thinking that everybody is out to get me—Black people included.

I was also agitated by the sharpness of my own memory. I thought to myself in a language that was not really my own: *Memory is an awful son-of-a-bitch full of content and past transgressions. Memory is an untold mystery. It is a scathing, hideous bringing back to life of all that was dead and buried.* Memory is a terror, much like a resurrection of Satan—Dante's *Dite*.

It is like the Apostle Paul's omnipresent evil, which is always raising its ugly head in the presence of the good and the beautiful. Memory is full of tears and sorrow. Sometimes, even a joy unspeakable, but more often than not, it is painful and unshareable. And yet, there are some things that we can never forget. Michel-Rolph Trouillot's statement that "the past has no content" is provocative but absurd to me. An absurdity that surpasses Albert Camus and Friedrich Nietzsche: *The Stranger* and *Beyond Good and Evil.* My own past is full of content. A past without content is like a future without hope. It is like a violation of memory's power to imagine a future. Allow me to speak for myself: *There are certain things about the past that I can never forget.* So, for me, there is no contentless past, and for that matter, "the past is never past." It's always just a thought away from rising up and speaking for itself—spilling its guts on the ground like a deer hit by a speeding Ford 350 pickup truck.

I am surprised by its clarity still lingering in my conscience. No, somewhat bitter, but not really surprised. I can still feel the sweltering sun shining bright in a cloudless sky on that particular Monday morning in late May. I was six years old, about to turn seven. It was the spring of 1959 on a narrow road in Southern Chesterfield County, Virginia—just a half mile from our small two-room clapboard house in Matoaca. Across the road was a large white plantation house sitting almost a half mile off the road, perched on a bluff, surrounded by hundreds of acres of corn, wheat, and barley. I was a child, but I understood the meaning of stark difference. That side of the road was pale white and rich-looking. You could tell by the sight of several dark golden palomino horses grazing, of irrigation waters flowing over the crop fields and the manicured lawn. The white folk were driving their glistening new Pontiacs and Cadillacs. They were the Briscolls, whose houses, land, and jobs represented white privilege. On the other side of the same road, the side where we lived, you could tell the difference in a moment's glance. We lived in a box, a two-room barnlike structure built by my father's own hands.

Anyway, my cousin and I were walking to the corner store during the coolest part of the scorching hot day. In order to get there, we had to pass through a clump of houses where several white children were playing in their yards. We were always told to stay on the public road and not to veer onto anyone's property because white folk didn't need much of an excuse to shoot and kill you or cause some bodily harm to a Black boy, not during those days of Jim Crow. This was only a few years after fourteen-year-old Emmett Till's murder for saying "Hey Baby" to a white store owner's wife in the Mississippi Delta. Two white men went on trial and were acquitted by a jury of their peers in less than an hour for a heinous crime that for much of the nation sparked the beginning of the modern civil rights movement. This was four months before Rosa Parks refused to give up her seat and before Martin Luther King Jr. led the Montgomery Bus Boycott that helped to change the mind of the South and the nation. I remember these things because my daddy read the newspaper like it was the Bible, and he kept up with the evening news religiously. As a matter of fact, my daddy insisted that we not leave the "home place" while he was off at work. But, because boys will be boys, I was eager to join my cousin in our mile walk to Sadler's country store. It was just over the hill at the end of the road. So close to where we lived; yet, it was a whole world away.

As soon as we reached the top of the hill we knew that we were in white folks' territory. Over the hill was the danger sign for us because it marked the clear boundary between leaving the area where Blacks lived and entering into the white zone. As we passed the little cluster of houses where poor whites lived, three little rascals, playing in the yard, saw us walking on the main road. They moved to the edge of their property to taunt and harass us: "Niggers, go home." This was my first exposure to the word *nigger*. "Niggers, go home," they yelled and stuck up their middle fingers as we slowly came in full view. A double insult, with hand and mouth racism and vulgarity, spoken with a unified voice that threatened us less than a half mile from where we lived. My cousin, who was a few years older than I, whispered to me, "Just don't say a word. Ignore the little bastards, unless they come onto this road or hit us with rocks. And if they do try to hit us, then we will fight like hell. No white boy is going to get away with hitting me." My older cousin was bad.

"I'll kick their ass," my cousin said, bold with anger and determination. I was empowered by his blind courage. I didn't wear my feelings on my shirtsleeve, but internally I was just as angry as he. I think. Maybe even a bit more scared. The fact is Blacks were made to stand in fear by custom and by law, and I was a child. The sad truth is I was only six years old and didn't know what all the angst was about.

"Niggers, Black niggers, go back to Africa," they said over and over again until we got out of their sight and hearing range. We were now almost at the corner store, where Matoaca Road intersected with River Road. This was the heart of Ku Klux Klan country. I later learned that their local headquarters was just up the road a piece and off the beaten path about a half mile down a long footpath. We had twelve empty Coca-Cola bottles to redeem for one or two cents each. This was enough for us to purchase some candy and to buy ourselves a soda. At the time, a bottled Coke was six cents and most of the candy, like a jawbone breaker or a sugar daddy or lollipop, was one or two cents each. A dollar could purchase a lot back then. For a poor boy like me, a dollar might as well have been a hundred. On that day I certainly did walk a mile for a dollar, although it cost me more than it was worth. It cost me my childhood innocence. After that experience of being called *nigger*, my life would never be the same because I have not been able to forget it—fifty years later.

We made our purchases and then headed back down what seemed like the long road toward home. We had almost forgotten that we again had to pass by the same little white boys until one of them yelled, "Niggers, go home," and began to spit at us and throw rocks at us. All we could do was speed up and walk faster as we held on to our sodas and candy. God knows we didn't want to do anything to make us drop our goodies.

I got a terrible butt whipping that night because my daddy was adamant about us staying put when he was at work. My mother told him about my little adventure of mischief and disobedience. I can hear her even today as she told Daddy, "Richard, James Henry walked to the store today. He knew he was supposed to stay in the yard, but he was hardheaded." Hardheadedness was the name for any disobedience. My daddy was furious and, without asking any questions, ordered me to get the "strap"—or was it a "switch"?—so that I could receive my just punishment. Daddy was a big man with large, wide hands and broad shoulders. He was too big and strong to whip a six-year-old boy. After that awful whipping, I seldom disobeyed Mother and Daddy again. But I could not figure out why such harsh punishment was rendered for such a small, insignificant infraction. In my eyes, the punishment far outweighed the crime. What could I possibly know at such a young age about America? If I didn't know anything else, there is one thing I did know: that was the day when I was first called a nigger.

That day I learned one of life's worst lessons—that Black people are hated by some because of the color of their skin. And my learning it so early was tragic, yet profound. To come to self-consciousness by realizing that otherness can never be escaped because of one's dark skin slapped me squarely in the face that very day. Talk of diversity and equality is always suspect to me. It sounds like Orwellian doublespeak. Propaganda. "It just don't seem equal if you are Black." It might eventually come to be. So, I still refuse to be too cynical or too hopeless. Beautiful Black chocolate-colored skin, smooth as a milkshake, and yet, so hated. For what reason? I appeal to Socrates, Plato, and Aristotle. I appeal to the daughters of Zeus. No, I state my case to Zeus himself. I appeal to the Daughters of Thunder: Jarena Lee, Julia A. J. Foote, Harriet A. Baker, and Florence Spearing Randolph. I appeal to YHWH. To *Elohim*. To *Adonai*. I appeal to Moses and to the God of Abraham, Isaac, and Jacob. Please tell me it isn't so. It's an illusion. It's a dream. An awful dream. I ask myself, Why? What drives this insanity? What propels this irrationality by the architects of Enlightenment's rationalism and empiricism? Tell me. Please tell me. I ask Mark Twain and Joseph Conrad: *Why do you use the word* nigger *so much? So flippantly. So cavalier-like. So wrenchingly and unashamedly.* Somebody tell me. Explain it to me so that, maybe, I too can understand. Is that too much to ask for? To hope for?

There was more to think about. My mind kept vectoring toward the past. I thought of the struggles of my childhood and youth. I thought about being bullied in high school and how it did not stop me from loving school. I thought about the year I graduated and got my first job that summer in the tobacco factory. I thought of everything in a way that would help me keep my sanity. The struggles of life are not linear. Life goes up and down, back and forth in a single moment. Some days I travel for fifty-three years through mountains of memories and regrets. And some days I travel nowhere at all, just sitting in class with my mind somewhere else.

Chapter 4

During the fourth week of class, Mark Twain's *Adventures of Huckleberry Finn* forced me to think long and hard about how today's young Black people mimic his language, by using a hybrid form of the word *nigger*. Not even the white rapper from Detroit, Eminem, has ventured to do what Mark Twain does. Twain's mastery of the Black Southern dialect is at least equaled by Eminem's mastery of the Black rap and hip-hop dialect. Without visuals, Eminem would be presumed Black. The only indicator that Eminem is not Black is the fact that he never uses any variation of the word *nigger* in any of his rap music because he grew up in the ghetto. As a white rapper, he understands that this racial epithet is completely off-limits for whites. This is reverse irony. It is true that Eminem sounds and acts Black, but in America and the world, he is not Black. He is still white, and he has the skin color, the money, and the recognition to prove it. Acting and sounding Black, even wearing a hoodie, like Trayvon Martin, have never spelled death for a white person in America.

I must confess that the course professor and I were about the same age, with similar backgrounds in the humanities. So, I was always overinterpreting and hyperanalyzing almost every word that Mark Twain used. I had an insatiable hunger for understanding the text in my own way. I was expressing and working out my own feelings of tension and strife as I read the words spilling from Twain's pen.

A few years ago, I tagged along with my wife to the World Reading Conference in San Jose, Costa Rica. As I was waiting for her to come out of a seminar session, I struck up a conversation with a young man who was also accompanying his wife. I had told him that I was writing a book on my experience with the word *nigger* as used by Mark Twain and in Black culture, especially in hip-hop. He was a former marine who lived and worked in Baltimore.

"Anthony Brown, age forty-one," he said to me as he extended his hand in a brotherhood shake. He was fifteen years younger than me. A random meeting in Central America between two Black men from the United States, in a reading conference hotel lobby surrounded by people from all over the world: teachers, school principals, college reading professors, authors, and literacy coaches. After talking about the difference in complexion of Costa Ricans who come from the Caribbean side and those on the Pacific and inland part of the country, we began to talk about hip-hop and its use of the forbidden word *nigger*.

"So, what do you think about how rap and hip-hop have globalized the word *nigger*?" I asked.

"Hip-hop defines itself on its own terms. It has almost become messageless," he said.

"You think so?" I intoned.

"Well, let's face it. The people who greenlight the movement are not Black. They are the movers and shakers of the record industry. Those who fund the movement are California and New York businesspeople. Corporate America."

"OK. That's true."

"It's what sells. The beat, the misogyny. This type of stuff."

"What about the word *nigger*? And, allowing this word to be used in song after song?" I asked.

"It's more complicated than what people say. Black folk had the audacity to try to turn the meaning of the word upside down. That says something."

"Yeah. But what about the history of the word? As a vile racial epithet or the essence or symbol of white supremacy?"

"That's the complication. Most Blacks in the US know what it meant. But those in other countries have no real connection to it, other than through rap and hip-hop music and language."

"That's the danger," I said. "That's a problem with Black folk calling themselves *niggaz*. The history cannot be undone. And it cannot be explained fully to those who don't know."

I began to think more about it, as we stepped out of the grand lobby into the hot sun and went our separate ways.

A couple of years earlier while sitting in the baggage claim area of Houston's Intercontinental Airport, I overheard two Black and two Latino youths talking about their lives. Their language was unfiltered and laced with profanity and the cavalier use of the word *nigger* or its hybrid, *nigga*. I couldn't believe what I was hearing. I was confused and surprised because they used the word so freely in referring to each other as well as to others who were the subject of their conversation. And, unlike me, they didn't care who heard them.

"Nigger, don't be so goddamn stingy with those chips."

"Come on nigger, you just a greedy ass mutha fucka."

"Nigger, you can kiss my Black ass."

I realized that this demotic language usage by Blacks in the presence of whites and Latinos is a new reality embedded in popular culture, and young African Americans and other minorities have a different understanding of the forbidden word than I do. I didn't think the word should be used by non-Blacks, and especially whites, in the presence of Blacks, because I interpret that as racist and colonialist. But what do I know? Who am I to judge? Nevertheless, the use of the word *nigger* or *nigga* has taken on overtones that have fused a connection or disconnection between persons of different races and cultures. While the usage has been fused, the meaning is still unclear when used by Japanese, Chinese, French, Germans, Algerians, Egyptians, and others who have not had the common experience of oppression like African Americans—an experience rooted in American chattel slavery. To some, this doesn't matter. But, to me, it matters a lot because our history is a sacred memory that helps to shape our identity.

There is an appetite for the music that is felt all over the
world among different races, cultures, and socioeconomic
classes. Hip-hop seems to be unstoppable.

In a strange sense, rap was born long before its time. My first
memory of rap was when Muhammad Ali (aka Cassius Clay)
came on the television scene as a young twenty-one-year-old
boxer talking trash and talking pretty. And in this sense it was
born out of the resistance to the draft by Muhammad Ali, who
argued that he was a pacifist—a conscientious objector to the
violence of war. Ali's resistance to American hegemony and
the violence of the Vietnam War made him the focus of the news
media. He was a new Negro who did not fear the white man. He
did not hold his head down when he talked to white people. He
looked them directly in the eyes and spoke his mind without
apology. In many ways Muhammad Ali became the new symbol
of Black manhood and Black pride. He was the voice of resistance
and hope, so much so that every Black male I knew exhibited a
new confidence because of this young, handsome, self-assured
high school graduate from Louisville, Kentucky. He was strong
and could fight for the system and against the system and could
still talk pretty. In the language and spirit of Mark Twain's Huck
Finn, hip-hop music, and David Sedaris, "We Talk Pretty One
Day, yes we does. Dad blame it!"

Thinking about Ali now forced me to reckon with hip-hop
and rap music and the way these Black rappers talked. One
thing led to another. Reading Huckleberry Finn caused me to
think about contemporary issues and how young Blacks also
use the forbidden word. The reading raised a lot of questions
and a lot of anguish and a good bit of ambivalence. I began to
think more about growing up as a Black boy and how Richard Wright's autobiography novel Black Boy inspired me and
became the single most influential book in my life.

Chapter 5

Daddy and Uncle C. F. and 'em came home early that particular day. They never had the time, the money, or the mindset to just sit around talking trash and shooting the breeze. Certainly not on a workday. A weekday. But this day was different. Something I cannot explain was happening in the soul of America. I could feel it in the air. Like the spirit, and the sound of Stevie Wonder, the answer was blowing in the wind. Out of nowhere, Uncle John said, "We been down long enough now. We done paid our dues." He sounded sad and sorrowful. Rebellious, not pitiful. Marvin Gaye's music was playing in the background.

"Man, what are you talking about? You been smoking too much of that Wild Rabbit tobacco."

"I ain't been smoking not'ing. I'm talking about the fight."

The heavyweight boxing match. It was a sign of the times. The new mind of the South was emerging with a new consciousness of the wrongs that had become commonplace.

This language of rebellion and freedom became clear to me as the day unfolded. It was Tuesday, May 25, 1965. The fight was being broadcast from an arena in Lewiston, Maine—Muhammad Ali versus Sonny Liston. Ali was a rebel. A Black Muslim: *Salaam alaykum.*

In our neighborhood, there were only one or two TVs, and we didn't have one. But the heavyweight boxing championship fight was about to come on, so we all gathered around the small black-and-white television at my grandmother's house. Since there was no room for me to sit, I stood against the wall trying to make myself comfortable. I was one of about twenty-five people crammed into the small TV room. It was stifling hot. The windows were hoisted and the one electric fan buzzed, but the temperature continued to swell as the room filled up. We sucked every ounce of cool air out of the small room. I was sweating so much somebody handed me a small fan from the local funeral home. It was their way of advertising their services. I prayed that no one would have a heat stroke and drop dead. Crouched on the floor, standing against the wall, and seated on the beaten-down couch, we could hear the announcer, Howard Cosell, jabbering and pontificating—trying to predict what was going to happen. His mouth was running more than a mile a minute as his doubts and biases seeped into every phrase of his commentary.

Howard Cosell was boxing's most omniscient voice. He knew everything about Ali's history and training and often peppered him with questions and comments that seemed designed to trip the champ up and make him sound like a fool. But Ali was more than up to the task. His rhythmic speech was more poetic and alluring than the robotic and manufactured cadence of Howard Cosell. Howard Cosell was loathed in our small community because we thought he antagonized Muhammad Ali. He was combative and condescending. But Ali was a skilled verbal expert in the language of the masses. And, despite all of Howard Cosell's efforts to humiliate and lacerate him with his sharp tongue, Ali always had a retort—complete with Shakespearean rhyme and African rhythm. It was like the beat of a drum. The timing. The syncopation. The intimidating size of Muhammad Ali. The height. The weight. The muscles. He was too strong, too bold, and too confident for the little scrawny man. More than that, he was sharp and witty. Linguistically and semantically, Ali was Langston Hughes and Richard Wright. He was Malcolm X and Martin Luther

King Jr. all rolled up into a "single garment of destiny." And he would have the last word "by any means necessary." The left hook or the right jab. The poem or dialogue. It was the poet, the sweet-talking rapper from Louisville, Kentucky, against Liston, the brusque former prisoner and son of a sharecropper from Arkansas. Cosmopolitan versus backwater. Photogenic versus the bland everyday-looking Joe. The self-proclaimed pretty-face heavyweight fighter who could "float like a butterfly and sting like a bee" caused a stir in our little self-contained neighborhood. He was cocky and strong, tall and lean, a guy who could talk fast and pretty. In his mind, and in the minds of many others, he had a pretty face, pretty hands, and pretty feet. "I am pretty," he said. "Look at my pretty face." To some, he was the epitome of masculinity and charm. He had the face of a model and the body of a Greek god. The women and teenage girls drooled over his smooth, muscular, brown-skinned body. My sisters, my aunts, and my female cousins all thought he was sexy. Manly. Cocky. To others, he was conceited. Egotistic. Arrogant. There was no argument that he was lightning fast. A perfect poster boy for boxing as the equal opportunity sport. A ticket seller. An entertainer. A television sensation. Ali was the man! The new Black man!

Everybody on our place was talking about Ali—this new Joe Louis. "Our place" was a stretch of property between two hills on Matoaca Road. Indian country. Just a few miles from the banks of the Appomattox River, which separates the southern border of Chesterfield County from Dinwiddie County in central Virginia. About one hundred acres of farmland and forest bordered by a small, shallow creek. This is God's country. The fresh smell of blackberries, watermelon, persimmons, honeysuckle, and wildflowers hovered in the morning dew and settled on the grass and the leaves of the trees. I loved the land and cherished the freedom we enjoyed. A freedom to roam, to

play, and to sleep under the stars. This was community property purchased by my paternal grandparents and their ten adult
children when they moved from Oxford, North Carolina, like
a flotilla of nomads. All of my father's brothers and sisters and
their spouses lived on this property in small shanty-like houses.
It was like a compound. In the center of the land was the Big
House, where my grandmother lived. We played for hours in
the front yard or sat on the front porch all day long when we
were not working in the tobacco and corn fields. Mainly on
Sundays, or when somebody was sick. We were porch people
who could do as we pleased because the house was a quarter
of a mile off the main road, hidden from everything except the
birds, the squirrels, and the light of the sun.

The Big House was not really so big. It was in fact quite small.
Still, it was bigger than any other house on the family place.
The Big House had about seven rooms. It had an upstairs and
four brick fireplaces. It looked like a midwestern wood-frame
farmhouse. There was a cemetery out front under a grove of
large cedar trees. Names of folk who lived during the Civil War
were etched in the headstones. My grandparents had bought
the property from a group of white antebellum farmers. In my
world, this house was B-I-G because our little house, like all the
rest, had two rooms. We all slept in one room and cooked and
ate in the other. It was there in the Big House that everybody
gathered for almost everything. We had prayer meetings there.
We held our own church services. I remember one late summer evening we were all gathered for a prayer meeting to which
my Uncle Joe had invited one of his many friends to preach a
sermon after the singing and praying. The visitor was a little,
stubby white man whose name now escapes me. A jackleg. Rev-
erend somebody. The atmosphere was charged with the Holy
Spirit. It was a hallelujah time going on in the Big House. As
this blue-eyed evangelical white man with a southern twang

in his voice began to open his Bible, he asked a question of all of us—loud and clear: "Who among y'all gathered under the sound of my voice believe that if you were to die tonight you would go to heaven?"

"I believe it. Sure I'm going to heaven," said my daddy.

"Yes, sir. I know I'm going to heaven," echoed my Uncle C. F.

"Raise your hands high and stand up so we can see you," he said.

When Daddy and Uncle C. F. stood up, I was shocked. Flabbergasted. I couldn't believe it. Everybody else sat in their seats. How could these two guys be so sure of their eternal destiny? What made them think that their lives and their faith were so strong? I remember that particular night because their reaction to the question was beyond my childhood imagination. I saw them so differently than the way they saw themselves. These two guys were the toughest, strongest, most hard-working, no-nonsense folk in my life. My daddy would whip us in a split second and work us like slaves from sun-up to sundown. Daddy was a big muscular guy. About five foot eleven, weighing more than 220 pounds. He was solid as a rock—and the unofficial bouncer whenever there was trouble between his brothers or between his sisters and their husbands. Daddy was the man. One day our mule, Rodie, was acting stubborn and crazy and in one instance kicked at Daddy rather than obey his command. Daddy, with his bare fists, knocked the mule out cold. Just like Ali, who pummeled his opponents for daring to step into the ring, Daddy too was a strong man.

And Daddy was the quiet and calm one. Uncle C. F. was feisty and cocky. He was small in stature, but he was like a bantam rooster. He was verbose, manly, and confident. He would challenge us and double-dare us to try to wrestle him. Out of love and respect I never took him up on his wager. But, when I think about it, it was more than love and respect. It was the fear of losing because I knew he was a strong man trained by the US Navy. I said something smart-alecky to him one day when he was on a tirade. We were in the tobacco field and I had done something that didn't meet his satisfaction. He was pissed off by my youthful hubris.

"Are you a Harris?" he bellowed.

"I don't know what I am," I responded.

"A Harris don't act like that."

"For all I know, I may not be a Harris."

"What do you mean, boy? I ought to hit you in your mouth for talking foolish like that."

"I could be a Goode or a Williams for that matter," I continued.

"Richard, that boy has lost his damn mind. He's too smart for his own good."

My favorite uncle was hot-tempered. His choleric behavior was evident that day. He was mad because I had talked back to him in a way that cast doubt on my paternity and on his patriarchal privilege. I had learned some of my behavior from him because I was always around him. His ways were my ways. His taunts were my taunts. I had learned from the master intimidator, the one whose mouth alone could create fear in anyone who was weak or shy. But this was all a façade, because I learned that night at the Big House that my beloved uncle C. F. was a God-fearing man who didn't mind singing and testifying and confessing his faith and his fears.

I'm probably exaggerating, but that's how I saw it back then. I misinterpreted my daddy's and my uncle's toughness as meanness and undeserving of inheriting the Kingdom of God. So, I was blown away by the immediacy of their response that night. There was no hesitation or trepidation. Theirs was a New Testament faith, which is the "substance of things hoped for, the evidence of things not seen." My daddy and Uncle C. F. were heaven-bound long before I came to understand it. Their salvation was real. The Apostle Paul's admonition to the church at Rome had taken hold in their souls. Salvation and the afterlife demanded no long theological treatise, no dogmatic defense or explanation. It required a simple *yes, I believe*, which was the meaning of it all. The Bible teaches the righteousness that comes from faith:

> *Do not say in your heart,*
> *Who will ascend into heaven . . .*
> *or who will descend into the abyss?*
> *The word is near you,*
> *on your lips and in your heart . . .*
> *because if you confess with your lips that Jesus is Lord and*
> *   believe in your heart that God raised him from the dead,*
> *   you will be saved . . .*
> *For, everyone who calls upon the name of the Lord shall be saved.*

Bless their sweet spirits and their gentle souls as they now rest in the eternal peace of God. Every time I think of them both I begin to cry because I realize that my daddy and my uncle were blessings to me.

My daddy and his brothers had not been avid boxing fans. But now it seemed they were. Daddy sat on the edge of his seat or jumped up in the middle of a round spouting words that showed another side of his peaceful and placid personality: "Hit him. Come on, knock him out. Kill him." Daddy became loud and passionate. No cussing or swearing, though—just flexing muscles and reflexing limbs. He would mimic Ali. Every time Ali would jab, Daddy would jab. When Ali would gyrate, Daddy would do the same. I stood away from him during the fight because anyone standing too close to him could easily get hit and hurt pretty bad.

Young Muhammad Ali was the new Negro—a Southern, confident, loud-mouthed, rhythmic preacher-like poet who could stand toe-to-toe with any boxer or sports commentator. Well, on this night all of the hoopla that had preceded and accompanied the anticipated fifteen-round fight came to an abrupt halt in a disappointing few seconds. The opponent was down on the canvas. Knocked out—KO'ed before the first round could hardly begin. It was a shock. Some said the fight was fixed because it happened so fast. All of us in the cramped, jam-packed room felt the power of the left jab and the swift right hook that took Sonny Liston down. It was like lightning had struck him beside the head. His knees wobbled and his contorted mouth hung open. His legs and arms were flailing as he fell to the floor. This was swift and decisive. We were all dumbfounded. First minute, first round. The fight was over before I could even sit down. I could hear my brother John say, in a voice laden with melancholy and sadness, "The fight done come and gone."

Chapter 6

The day, at age fifty-three, that I opened the pages of Mark Twain's epoch-making *Adventures of Huckleberry Finn* for the first time in a graduate-level class where I was the only Black, I knew I was in for a fight over words, language, history, and culture. Let's not forget that I'm the product of segregated schools, where Twain's *Adventures of Huckleberry Finn* was never on the reading list. I was a tenured full professor at Virginia Union University, a historically Black school in Richmond that had stood since 1865. The school had its beginning in Lumpkins Jail—a depot in Shockoe Bottom used to house slaves as they got off the boat at the Port of Richmond. The school has a well-established and prominent seminary that has been training ministers and some of America's best preachers and pastors for over a hundred years. As a teacher there, I was earning little money, but I was dedicated to helping Black adults and youth become scholars, leaders, and independent thinkers. Maybe I'm too dedicated and too hard on mediocrity. My students often complain that I require too much reading in my courses. I don't think so. I set the bar high because it was set high for me by professors at Virginia Union. A master of divinity degree is an academic badge of honor—a sign of readiness for leadership in ministry. More than that, it means that you are a certified preacher who has something meaningful to say to the people of God. It means that you are a public intellectual worthy of addressing the moral, economic, social, and political issues of the day. Many of my students come back years later to say "Thank you."

More importantly, I have been a pastor of Second Baptist Church (West End) in Richmond, Virginia for nearly thirty years and before that I was a pastor of Mt. Pleasant Church in Norfolk, Virginia. The Black Church is where my first love lies, and these are the people who have nurtured me from childhood. They have taught me and I have tried to be worthy of their love and support. It has been hard, because I have also been a contrarian, a brother, a father, a teacher, a friend, and confidant to both youth and adults. I have demonstrated the value and importance of schooling and education by staying in the classroom as a student and teacher. The church, more than the seminary, has been my laboratory and my own safe haven as well as a safe haven for hundreds of poor youth and adults in the community. I love the Black Church in all its complexities. Those on the outside and the inside know of its power and importance to Black identity, strength, and survival. It remains central to Black life and the Black preacher is at the helm of the ship. Twain on the other hand didn't care too much for religion. He made fun of it as often as possible.

For more than twenty years I had been teaching the craft of writing and delivering sermons to experienced pastors and beginning students. I, too, was a preacher. None of this was an elixir for the pain I experienced in hearing the word *nigger* over and over again as the white students in that graduate course read out loud. So, yes, I knew that, like the fight between Ali and Liston, this would be a tough battle. This would be a slug-fest between me and my consciousness, between me and the professor, between me and the other students, between me and the novel itself. We were in the fifth week of class and from the first day, I felt the stinging blow of the professor and students trying to explain Mark Twain's use of the word *nigger*. I had taught myself to appear stoic and restrained by reading and studying most of my life. I had been in school for what seemed like an eternity, but I still was not ready to hear white folk use the forbidden word as if it were okay. There was probably no malice or mischief intended by any of them. At least I didn't think so. It was more like indifference on their part, as if I weren't even in the room. That was worse than malice. I felt like the main character in Ralph Ellison's *Invisible Man*. I was the spook at the door. Every time I heard the forbidden word, I felt as if a boxer like Muhammad Ali had punched me in the head and knocked me to the floor. It was the sting of the blow that caused the trauma to my body and soul. I was in a fight with myself and everybody around me. And I was being battered and bruised every time I heard the word *nigger*. My immunity built up to the point where I was no longer angry, but I was still troubled and my body was bruised.

Don't get me wrong. I love the way Mark Twain uses most American words. I marvel at how he crafts a phrase or a sentence. But I also hate his use of the forbidden word in *Adventures of Huckleberry Finn*. I don't think *hate* is too strong a word! It shows passion and self-esteem in this case, and it leads to sanity, not violence. I imagine that if the venerable Samuel Clemens had somehow stepped over the boundary of mortality and lived beyond 1910 into this present era, he might very well express a mutual respect toward me. Any author willing to send his dear protagonist Huck Finn all the way to hell on behalf of one of my African American ancestors is certainly worthy of my acclamation. This is the love that I am talking about. I think Huck loved Jim and I know Jim loved Huck, because Black people have a strange love of whites. Yes, Black people love white people. However, when that dear protagonist exists amid pages that harbor one of the vilest words in the English lexicon, my acclamation plummets. Furthermore, when that same author—whose letters and critical acclaim carry an Oxford stamp of approval (albeit honorary)—weaves this vile word into his greatest work more than two hundred and eleven times, my acclamation turns into disdain.

The German Nobel Prize–winning author Günter Grass

reminds us in *Peeling the Onion*, "Even if an author eventually becomes dependent upon the characters he creates,
he must answer for their deeds and misdeeds." Mark Twain
then must answer for the deeds and misdeeds of Huck, Pap,
Aunt Sally, Miss Watson, Jim, the Grangerfords, the Shepherdsons, the King, the Duke . . . and even the Mississippi
River. Most of all, he must answer for the use of the word
nigger plastered on almost every page of the book.

I am not sure why Twain's use of this vile racial epithet
unsettles me so. I know that irony and satire permeate the book,
but that knowledge doesn't take away the sting of white folks'
use of *nigger*. I can't get comfortable with that. It made me feel
funny. I felt that I was betraying the Black race by simply being
in the room where the forbidden word was read or recited every
day. Black people understand irony and satire at a deeper level
than most folk because they have three hundred years of experience seeing themselves caricatured. I suppose my quest would
have been endangered had I ventured such an evaluation earlier in my life. I know I would not have been able to handle it. I
would have been too emotional, overcome by tears. I can hardly
handle it now. The truth is hard to tell and even harder to face.

Sitting there week after week forced me to think about difficult
things. And, not just me because my presence in the room, my jabs
against racism, and my constant interrogation of Mark Twain's use
of *nigger* caused everybody to think twice about their assumptions
that Twain was not a racist and *Adventures of Huckleberry Finn* was
as wonderful as Ernest Hemingway had proclaimed. But, that's not
all. It caused me to question my own assumptions and biases. It
made me realize that there were some folk in the seminar who were
almost as sensitive as I was to the word *nigger*. And, these folk
were not Black like me. They were white. I said "almost as sensitive,"
but what I mean is that they were empathetic toward me because
they could never know what it feels like being Black in America.

Chapter 7

The cigarette smoking by the young people in the class caught me off my watch. It was déjà vu because I had smoked Kool cigarettes until my first son was born in 1982. It's a powerful addiction. There were at least four or five students who spent every fifteen-minute break sitting on the banister of the porch or on the front steps smoking. I didn't know what to make of it because scientists had proven long ago that smoking causes all kinds of illnesses and death. It was 2006, not the 1870s when Twain was writing *Adventures of Huckleberry Finn*. And yet, the class had its own manifestations of Huck Finn—those who smoked in spite of the known dangers to themselves and others. I reckon that danger has never stopped folk from doing something harmful. I thought of Sigmund Freud's "death instinct" and the fact that he had smoked himself to death. Twain, however, felt that preaching and praying were likely more dangerous than smoking. He understood white folk's religion as a sham and a danger to freedom.

Huck Finn loved smoking, which is seen throughout the book. You can't turn the pages without encountering Huck and Jim desiring to smoke or actually lighting up. I was curious about this because smoking had played such a major role in my own family life. My uncle died from lung cancer, my father died from heart disease, my mother died from colon cancer, and my sister died from heart disease—all within the past twenty years. All of these deaths were related directly or indirectly to smoking, and yet almost half of my classmates in the seminar on Huck Finn also smoked. Nicotine addiction, like other drug addiction, is a scourge that plagues our society. This was irony par excellence.

As soon as you open the book, three pages into chapter one, you are lured into the smoke zone:

> Pretty soon I wanted to smoke, and asked the widow to let me. But she wouldn't. She said it was a mean practice and wasn't clean, and I must try not to do it anymore. That is just the way with some people. They get down on a thing when they don't know nothing about it. Here she was a bothering about Moses, which was no kin to her, and no use to anybody, being gone, you see, yet finding a power of fault with me for doing a thing that had some good in it. And she took snuff too; of course that was all right, because she done it herself.

Smoking was not something that I didn't "know nothing about." I was not like Huck's foster mother, the widow Douglas, because I knew a whole lot about smoking. In class that day, we talked about the fact that there are lots of references to Huck's smoking throughout the book and the fact that Huck took pride in smoking while Mark Twain's in-laws were against it. It wasn't long before I began to think about the summer I worked in the tobacco factory: Brown and Williamson Tobacco Company.

During my sophomore year in high school, Joseph Bolling, the class bully, sat directly behind me and pushed the handle of his switchblade knife against my back and whispered, "You need to shut up. You are too smart for your own good." I was shaking with fear. This man was a lunatic who put terror in my soul. He was grown and I was a child. The bully, who was eighteen years old in the ninth grade, stood a whole foot above me and weighed three times what I weighed. I was only thirteen and very skinny, weighing less than 120 pounds and standing at five feet, seven inches tall. Compared to him, I was a tumbleweed. I was a sprig, facing an oak tree. The fear I felt was obvious to Joseph, although there were others whom he picked on, I felt alone in my agonizing predicament. I can still hear his threatening taunts: "If you answer another question in here, I am going to stab you in the back with this knife." I began to fear for my life. So I quit being smart. Not that I was so smart in the first place.

In high school I never really liked English literature or the study of *Beowulf* or the poetry of Percy B. Shelly or Shakespeare. But I memorized Shakespeare's eighteenth sonnet:

Shall I compare thee to a summer's day?
Thou art more lovely and more beautiful:
Rough winds do shake the darling buds of May,
And summer's lease hath all too short a date

How romantic those words sounded. I practiced them by flattering girls every time I got a chance. Some girls thought these words "corny" and too rehearsed, but they were still impressed with my poetic flair. I thought I sounded like a poet. The connection was gradually being made. Romance is a natural phenomenon. Like love, it is a powerful emotion. Shakespeare had touched my heart and soul, but not in the same way the experience of reading Richard Wright's *Black Boy* had. That's where I found my spiritual place. I could relate to the poverty, the mischief, and the rebellion: the struggle of Blackness. That book changed my life. It was the first time I studied a book by a Black writer in our all-Black English classes. It was 1968, a few months before Martin Luther King was assassinated. It was thirteen years after Emmet Till, a fourteen-year-old Black boy, was murdered in Money, Mississippi, for whistling at the wife of a white store owner in the rural, backwater Mississippi Delta. Some say he said, boyishly, "Thank you, baby," to her as a response to a dare by his cousins and friends. Anyway, the white folk of that country town murdered him, placed a seventy-five-pound cotton gin fan around his neck, and dumped his mangled body into the Tallahatchie River. This was a terrorist act. This was the America I grew up in. I also read Claude Brown's memoir, *Manchild in the Promised Land*, which really pulled me in to a new self-awareness. I was hooked on literature that connected with my own experience as a Black boy. But, reading this literature was not "cool" in high school. It was dangerous to my physical health. So, I put it on the back burner until later. Much later.

There was more to this fear syndrome that engulfed me. I was also afraid of the fact that if my father found out that I allowed myself to be bullied, he would be upset and would punish me for being what he characterized as "afraid and weak." My daddy always said "stand up and be a man. I'm not raising you to be scared and weak." I interpreted this to mean "Don't be a chicken!" or "Don't be a sissy!" So, I was afraid at school and afraid to go home and tell anyone. I always wanted to please my mother and father more than anyone or anything else because my love for my mother and father outweighed my fears. Love and fear are two strong emotions that can easily be confused with each other. With my father, I think in retrospect, that love was more dominant than fear. That's not always the case. Fear is sometimes the dominant factor in relationships—marriages, families, with friends, and with lovers.

While I was in high school, there were only six or seven males registered in the College Preparatory Curriculum and I was one of them. We took foreign languages, math analysis, chemistry, physics, biology, and a host of other subjects to get us ready for college. After struggling through these courses with some threats and discouragement, I proudly graduated with a college prep diploma in June of 1970. I turned eighteen that same week; I thought I was grown. So I "lit out" and got a job at the local tobacco factory—Brown and Williamson Tobacco Company in Petersburg, Virginia. I was so happy to be making money. Now I could help my parents and my nine siblings to eat a little bit better. It was all about having enough to eat. I could help my daddy so he would not have to struggle and work so hard. I was more than eager to begin my first day of work at a factory that ran twenty-four hours a day, seven days a week. The second shift, from three o'clock in the afternoon to eleven o'clock at night, was my lot. It was like night school, teaching young country boys like me how to seek pleasure and greed. It was culture shock. A world of Black workers resembling a plantation but getting paid for your labors and getting hooked on smoking. It was a system that worked for the company and for the local economy. Petersburg was thriving and dying all at the same time.

No one else in our immediate family had finished high school and I was the fifth child. One of my older sisters had died as an infant after contracting pneumonia in the late 1940s, before penicillin reached the poor Black people of the South. Her name was Averlee, and her spirit was kept alive by my mother and father—Carrie Anna Jones Harris and Richard Harris. Some say my daddy's first name was John, but he never used it, and I didn't even know it until he died in 1988. He really didn't like the name John for himself, although they named my oldest brother John Richard. Maybe that's why he didn't like it; I don't know the real reason. I do know that nobody ever called him John Richard. But when I saw the front cover of the funeral bulletin, I was surprised. It read "John Richard Harris Sr." Daddy's name had been changed by one of my wise siblings.

That summer at the factory was a real experience-based education. My job required no intellectual ability or skill but a lot of muscle and common sense. I was an automaton, lifting trays of cigarettes from an overhead conveyor and placing them on a machine that packaged them in small colorful packs of twenty, then placed ten twelve-packs into a carton. Well, that seemed to be simple enough. The only problem was that each tray of cigarettes weighed sixty pounds and I didn't weigh much more than that. Each machine held ten trays and could pack a tray in thirty seconds, or at least every minute. The conveyor belt with the trays full of cigarettes required a certain height and I barely met the height and weight requirement at a smidgen below five feet, seven inches tall and 118 pounds. I had to stretch and reach just to get the job done. At the end of the first night, I was exhausted from the bruising banter of the machine operator and the lifting of heavy trays of cigarettes. The machine operator was a brute who barked out orders to me between complaints to the foreman. "Don't let my machine get that low," he yelled. "What the hell is wrong with you? You are too goddamn slow. How in the hell did you get this job?" He went on and on in an effort to break my concentration and my spirit. One day, he got so pissed that he went to the foreman to lodge a formal complaint against me for being too slow and weak. My shoulders were sore. My arms and legs ached. My eyes were red from inhaling nicotine and menthol flavoring for eight hours, five days a week. The smell of tobacco saturated my skin, hair, and lungs. I got home about midnight and slept for twelve straight hours. By the time I woke up the next day, it was time to get ready to go back to work. This was hell. The factory was a culture shock for me. Women wore tight pants and low-cut blouses. There was cleavage, perfume, and flirtation on every aisle. Sex was in the air and on everybody's mind. Blacks and whites working together to produce one of the most enjoyable, addictive, yet toxic experiences in life: the filtered Kool cigarette. Every drag represented the pull of death on the human body. "Ashes to ashes, dust to dust" should have been printed on every pack as a warning by the Surgeon General. They were like the Black and Mild cigars of today. Each floor of the factory was devoted to a different brand of cigarette, and I worked on the third floor, where Kool was packed and boxed. I know it sounds crazy, but I felt cool and I actually thought I was Kool. Marketing's success. What a fool I was. This was the summer that I became addicted to Kool cigarettes, an addiction that lasted for the next fifteen years. Even today, many years later, I dream of smoking and wake up in a sweat gasping for air and praying that it's all a dream because I *never* want to smoke again. Never.

Everybody who worked as a tray handler was given a ten-minute break every hour. This was really a smoke break—a get-hooked-on-nicotine-and-other-unknown-drug-ingredients break—because the break room had several benches and a large bucket of free cigarettes in the four corners of the poorly ventilated, windowless room. At first, I didn't smoke. I was a tireless preacher against smoking to everyone in my family. During those days almost everybody smoked: Mother, Daddy, John, Marianna, Gloria, aunts, uncles, cousins, teachers, ministers, doctors, and lawyers. Oh, and all the church folk took their last puff as they entered the holy sanctuary on Sunday mornings, and as soon as the benediction was pronounced they couldn't wait to get outside to light up. Years after I lost the crusade against smoking, I too became an addict to nicotine. When I was a young minister intern in a Richmond church, a deacon would buy me a pack of cigarettes and give them to me on Sunday mornings after church. It was a part of the ethos of the community and the church. And since Richmond and Petersburg were the homes of Philip Morris USA and Brown and Williamson Tobacco Company, I'm surprised that there was not a marketing campaign to distribute free cigarettes at prayer meetings and Sunday schools at Black churches. I thank God that after each baptism every child nine and over wasn't given a pack of cigarettes as a part of his or her catechism. Imagine that as a rite of passage into the community of faith. Maybe it wasn't necessary, since many of the congregants also worked at the factory. Philip Morris and Brown and Williamson were bosom buddies. Partners in corporate crime. Oops, I mean corporate citizens, researchers, and scientists. The tobacco companies and the government worked hand-in-hand to turn all of America's youth and adults into nicotine-dependent drug addicts. Thinking about it, Pap Finn's drunken words come back to me: "Call this a govment."

During that summer at the factory, I met all kinds of people. The factory was not just a business; it was a culture of greed, lust, and hedonistic pleasure. Some were hustlers, loan sharks, gamblers, bailers, good-timers. One Thursday night soon after I got paid, a very buxom and sexy young lady came up to me and proposed to show me a good time. I'm sure I looked as horny as I felt. I was eighteen years old, at the pinnacle of the age of infinite sexual desire. The age of instant erections and "jacking off" or "choking the chicken." I remembered that when I was fifteen, I had stayed at home one day because I felt too sick to go to school. I thought I was in our little house alone when my mother opened the door and caught me doing it and admonished, "James Henry, stop playing with yourself." I was humiliated. Can you imagine being caught by your mother?

The buxom woman trying to get my money was on the brink of success. I was green and country to her and her sights were set on getting most of my hard-earned money under the guise of showing me a good time. A week's pay would have been blown away by the pleasure principle. I was no feckless fool, but I was caught in the middle of youthful desire and adult responsibility. My frail and weak body wanted to take her up on her offer, but I also wanted to keep my hard-earned money.

It was more cash than I had ever seen in my whole life: $156 a week after taxes. I could see her beautiful brown, smooth body through one eye and my daddy's face through the other. My daddy won that battle. I was a wimp, a scatty-scrimp of a man. I passed up the chance for pure hedonistic pleasure in order to help my family. I reasoned that there would be other chances to spend money on women. I have always been a bit too rational, too restrained—second-guessing my choices in life. And, God, have I made some bad choices.

I spent that entire summer in the factory, but when the last day of August rolled around the foreman asked all the summer help if we wanted to become permanent employees. Yes, was the resounding response by many who stayed on. This was their dream job. The money was too good for them to give up. They were driven by immediate satisfaction, which sometimes is one's only chance of happiness. But when he got around to me, I said, "I'm going to college in September; God knows I would like to stay here and work, but I can't." So in a matter of two weeks, I was back where I started—struggling to make ends meet. I had postponed immediate satisfaction for future fulfillment. I'm still not sure I made the right decision after all these years because an educated Black man as the leader of a Black church is still swimming upstream. Support is often tepid and lukewarm. People in the church are suspicious about too much book learning. They think it may quench the spirit. And besides, most church folks, the educated included, want the pastor to entertain them with nebulous ideas—nothing too heavy or challenging unless it's mediated by a joke or a lie. If laughter is the best medicine, then the Black minister is a doctor of medicine. The job was over and I was about to start classes at Virginia State College, to me the most prestigious school in the world because the world was not flat. It just had a very small radius.

A whole generation of youth were lured into tobacco addiction that summer. We got free cigarettes every hour and two packs of free cigarettes at the end of our eight-hour shift. Five days a week. Ten packs a week as a reward, a gift. This was the gift of death. Just be cool and smoke yourself to death: that's the message I got from that summer experience. But, I was too young to know or face the truth. I was invincible. I thought that I knew more than I really did know. The book of Proverbs and Socrates have warned that this is the mark of a fool. A young, invincible fool. I was enjoying the buzz from inhaling the addictive toxins—one puff at a time. I'm glad I gave up that job before it was too late. I felt a strange sorrow for those who were trapped in the culture of the factory for life. It was a life sentence. No, it was a death sentence. One puff at a time. As strange as it may seem, I liked the other benefits of working in the factory: a steady job, good money, and doing what everyone else did. It's so much easier to do what everyone else does no matter what it is. When the subject of my going to college came up, my aunt told my daddy that it was an absurd idea.

"Richard, look at that boy's hands. They are big and strong. Perfect for plowing the fields," she said.

My daddy said, "If he wants to go to college, I'm going to try to help him." My aunt didn't say anything else. She just looked at Daddy and shook her head in disgust and unbelief.

I remember standing in line for nearly eight hours to register for classes at Virginia State College in September 1970. It's a Black college ritual. I didn't really know what to major in because I hadn't thought that far in advance. Just being in college was a miracle from God, thanks to Senator Claiborne Pell, who helped to make it possible for poor people like me to attend college with the Pell Grant. And registration in a Black college is in itself such a challenge that getting through it is a lesson for life. Anybody who has ever attended a historically Black college or university knows exactly what I'm talking about. Everything is a struggle. All-day registration in the un-air-conditioned gym was the norm. This was a new frontier for me and my family. I knew that I didn't want to be a schoolteacher, and certainly I did not even consider becoming a preacher. These were the two most common professions for Blacks. And you didn't have to go to college to become a preacher. All you needed was to accept the call of God, and if you could sing, then you were qualified to be a preacher. Most Black preachers were jacklegs. Teaching was a different story. Most Blacks had to have college degrees, but in some localities, whites did not have to have a college degree to teach elementary school.

I reasoned that I would study business management. It sounded good and looked glamorous because all the people I knew—those who dressed up every day, drove nice cars, and seemed to be in charge of everything imaginable—were white businessmen and women. That was the formula for success. Everything important for as long as I could remember had been characterized as "business." My father would take a full bath, dress up, and put on his best clothes and his best persona to "do business, handle business." Business was everything that Daddy and Momma did that seemed to require extraordinary effort, cleanliness, and association with white folk and uppity Black people outside of the family. So, I reasoned that I would major in business administration at the only college I knew anything about: Virginia State College in Ettrick, Virginia.

The school was only about five miles from where we lived, and we had to pass it to go into town. It sat high on a hill above the Appomattox River. But for me it was much higher and farther away than five miles. It was a whole galaxy away. Professors, associate professors, assistant professors, lecturers, and instructors, all dressed up in their coats and ties looking like church folk every day of the week. I thought these were the smartest Black people I had ever encountered. Well, at least most of them. They knew something about everything and they had gone to some of America's most prestigious universities—schools that were north of the Mason-Dixon Line because, before the Civil Rights Act of 1964, Blacks could not attend schools like the University of Virginia or the University of Mississippi. These teachers were historians, biologists, physicists, mathematicians, philosophers, sociologists, and psychologists. Scholars, they were. I was highly impressed. Wow! I was walking in high cotton. Pap Finn would have died on the spot. Seeing all these free Black "po'fessors" who could vote would have killed him dead.

Imagine this too. For most of the sixties we didn't even have running water or a television in our house, so we had to go to my grandmother's house to feed my father's devotion to watching the national and local news. Every evening, around 6:00, we walked for about a quarter mile along the back path at the edge of the woods from our little frame house to my grandmother's house—the so-called Big House—to watch TV. My paternal grandmother, called "Pretty Mama" because, we were told, she would never come downstairs without being fully dressed or made up, died when I was about three years old. I vaguely remember her. She was a beautician trained in the art of looking pretty. "Beauty culture," they called it back then. Her house became the extended family's house, inherited by my father and all of his brothers and sisters, but my aunt and her husband and their children lived there as caretakers and heirs of the property.

The Harrises had come to Virginia from Oxford, North Carolina, around 1940 to farm the land. After a few years they began to marry some of the indigenous county residents. The Joneses. The Browns. The Turners. Almost everyone who got married, married somebody from one of these three families.

Cousins married one another. Kissing cousins. My closest relatives even today are either Harrises, Joneses, or Browns. On
one of the visits to the Big House, where the Browns lived, I
remember seeing on television the governor of the state of Alabama standing in the doorway of the registrar's office at the
University of Alabama to block the entrance of the first Black
persons to try to register for classes at this school—a citadel of
segregation and the symbol of white supremacy in the American South.

Governor George Wallace's behavior embodied what the
French philosopher Paul Ricoeur calls the "symbolism of evil."
The South—places like Birmingham, Selma, Memphis, and
Little Rock—were like war zones. Richmond, Virginia, was a
bit more genteel. Or maybe more schizophrenic or delusional.
Some of the Black citizens felt a certain kinship to white privilege and were a bit more cautious and attentive to proper social
etiquette. Reserved, but no less angry. A type of controlled fury
bubbled beneath the epidermis. Some places in the North, too,
were just as bad until the riots of 1967 in Newark, when Black
folks' anger and distress boiled over into the streets after years
of simmering. These were the places where white resistance
to integration was violent and vile in the land of freedom and
democracy. Southern governors were the worst kind of segrega-
tionists, and to some extent American Presidents Eisenhower,
Kennedy, Johnson, and Nixon needed a lot of prodding by Martin Luther King Jr., Malcolm X, and their followers. Black folk
loved Kennedy more than the others. But, to me, they all were
pretty much the same—beneficiaries of white privilege and the
economics of American slavery. They were the true American
elites. Not like the propagandist language former Senator Hil-
lary Clinton used to describe President Barack Obama during
the 2007 Democratic presidential campaign. Governor George
Wallace's dictum and motto "Segregation today, segregation

tomorrow, and segregation forever" characterized the spirit of many white citizens in America. It was a turbulent time, but it was my reality.

I spent my childhood and teenage years growing up in central Virginia, where the winters were often cold and cloudy and the summer's heat scorching. I usually turned two shades darker during the months of June, July, and August. We spent our days from sunup to sundown in the yard playing or in the tobacco field, planting, priming, seeding, and harvesting from May until October. The work was hard and the rewards were scarce. But we survived from year to year by the grace of God and the hard work of my daddy and mother.

One summer, a funny thing happened between May 30 and June 1, 1968. In less than a day's time, I met a new family member who arrived in the middle of the night. He was my grandfather's younger brother—Robert Harris. I always thought Uncle Robert looked like a slave. His skin was tough and Black as boot leather. He was stocky with a large potbelly the size of a fullgrown watermelon. He had beady eyes, no teeth, and a bald head with patches of solid white hair around his ears. He said he remembered slavery in North Carolina. I believed him too.

Around 1968, Uncle Robert came to live with my aunt Louise. My uncle Bernard, who was a jackleg preacher, businessman, and hustler, had brought him to the Big House one day without warning. Uncle Robert loved to drink warm beer. I was intrigued. Who drinks beer that has not been chilled?

"Uncle Robert, why do you drink your beer warm?"

"Well, son, I gets a bigger kick from it that way."

"You mean . . ."

"That's right, there is more buzz to it when it's warm. Don't give me no cold beer. Warm is how I likes it."

Uncle Robert had no front teeth. I remember seeing purple gums and being surprised that being toothless did not keep him from chewing on a chicken bone. Every Friday, Momma would cook fried chicken and fish: butter fish, spots, or croakers. Uncle Robert didn't live with us but he ate a lot of meals at our table. Daddy never turned anyone away. Sometimes he acted like we had more than we had. I was always hungry and felt a bit deprived because we barely had enough to feed the many mouths in our immediate family. But, for Daddy, all family was immediate. If you were present at suppertime, Daddy would make sure you ate. He was Mister Hospitality. My mother was the supportive wife who, like my siblings, also called my father "Daddy."

"Carrie, set a plate for Bob," he would say.

Every Friday evening, like clockwork, Uncle Robert walked the back path from my aunt's house down to our house, where he talked to Daddy, smoked cigarettes, and ate fried chicken, butter fish, and cornbread. He was my great uncle and Daddy's uncle from Oxford, Granville County, North Carolina. He lived in a room off to the side of the kitchen where he stored stuff that he had collected over the years. I shopped for everybody and he was no exception. I used to shop for him every week after I wrote the list of groceries: bread, sodas, cheese, crackers, sardines, potted meat, ginger ale, and Colt 45 Malt Liquor.

"Don't forget the beer," he would say before Daddy and I drove off. He drank one or two six-packs a week. The same brand. "Get me the one that has the kick to it," he intoned. Before Uncle Robert came to the place, drinking alcoholic beverages was forbidden. It was interesting to see my daddy and his brothers and sisters adjust their tolerance and remove the self-righteous prohibition against alcohol. Uncle Robert liberated all of us by making beer drinking acceptable. An amazing feat. Blood trumps tradition and creeds. By virtue of his age alone, he became the new lawgiver.

During the whole time he stayed on the place, I don't ever remember him going to church on Sundays or any other day.

Uncle Robert didn't believe in too much religion or anything like that. I thought he was an atheist or agnostic. He stayed to himself. Sitting under the big oak tree. Dozing. Seeing, but not seeing. Hearing, but not hearing, and pretending all the while to be disinterested in his surroundings. Playing possum was his gift. Also, he was pretty cantankerous and sly. As sly as a fox.

One day in the middle of summer, I got up earlier than usual, walked down to the Big House, and saw Uncle Robert untie Daddy's mule and shoo her off to roam. He did this out of sheer spite and evil. There is no other explanation for his clandestine action. I was afraid of the mule and Uncle Robert knew of my fear. A fear that he could not understand and did not seek to help me overcome. He would complain to me about it.

"You should be ashamed of yourself. As big as you are you shouldn't be scared of that mule."

"I'm not scared, I'm not," I said.

"Yes, you is. I can tell, boy," he said.

He was right and the mule was right. They both could sense my fear as clearly as if I were wearing a sign that said, "Look at me, I'm scared." They could smell my fear.

The mule loved to be free of the constraints of grazing in an assigned area. So she would often break away or get loose from the tree or stave. And boy would she run wild like a stallion. Sometimes she would cross the road onto the Briscolls' property, and other times she would run up the road like she was a Buick LaSabre or a Ford Mustang, refusing to move over for cars and trucks, causing havoc and fear up and down the road. People would blow their horns, yelling and cussing as they slowed down to keep from killing this crazy-ass mule. I would just let her run and rollick because I was afraid of her size and wildness. She was an untamed terror to a skimp like me. I had seen a horse fall down on my uncle and break his upper thigh and pelvis. I had also seen our mule kick my brother.

More than that, this mule weighed over twelve hundred pounds. And I was a skinny, scrawny teenage boy. Uncle Robert was right. I was embarrassed by the truth and unable to face my own fears. It was not natural for a farm boy to be afraid of an animal and the rigmarole of keeping it grazing in the right spot day after day. Animals were made to be mastered, controlled, or slaughtered. Animals on the farm had no rights. This was the sad truth. I had seen my daddy castrate and slaughter hogs, wring the necks of chickens, skin squirrels, and do whatever else needed to be done to put food on the table. I think we even cooked and ate a raccoon once! And, yet I was afraid of the mule. A mule that I was assigned to take out of the barn, walk to a grazing field, and tie to a stave. While I did this day after day and week after week, I never overcame the basic, deeply embedded fear, and the mule could sense it, because in her own way, she would taunt me and dare me to try to control her wanton ways. Huckleberry Finn and Jim would have made me look like milquetoast. They were pretty fearless.

Chapter 8

When I was growing up, we didn't have many books in our house. The only books we had were textbooks from school and a very used Bible with some pages missing. We were too poor to buy books on our own. We could seldom buy enough food. I was always hungry. Our house was a two-room sanctuary of innocence and ignorance. We were an extended family in the best and worst sense of the word. Everybody was family: aunts, uncles, cousins, brothers, and sisters. While we knew love, we were too poor to really know what poverty was and too proud to admit it. To tell the truth, I had to go to school to learn about how poor we really were.

There was a bit of incest among cousins and probably some bestiality too. My sister told me that she saw two of our cousins kissing one day. And, I witnessed a few things myself taking place behind the barn or in the cornfield.

We also knew who was zooming whom among our aunts and uncles and cousins. Or, at least we heard secret things about our aunts and uncles and their extramarital affairs. Stuff that people delight in: sex, lies, drinking liquor, gossip. Aunt so-and-so was sleeping with Mr. X, or Uncle so-and-so had one family on Matoaca Road and another family in Petersburg or Chesterfield. There was a lot of hanky-panky going on beyond the façade of church-going piety and innocence. When the first telephone arrived on the place, at the Big House, the phone rang one day and the voice on the other end said, "I want to speak to my daddy. Is my daddy there?"

"You must have the wrong number. What number were you trying to call?" my aunt asked.

"526–8043. I know this is the right number."

"OK. Who did you say you wanted to speak to?"

"My daddy. Is he there?"

"Who is your daddy? What's your daddy's name?" Click. The phone went dead.

Our house had no electricity and no running water. It had no indoor plumbing and no central heat. We used to draw water from the well at the Big House and carry it in buckets to our house, along the back path about a quarter mile away. It was a pretty deep well, about twenty to twenty-five feet. I used to lean over it and look down into the cavernous dark hole. Sometimes, I'd drop a rock into the well and wait to hear it reach the bottom. Its echo sounded so distant, I imagined what it would feel like to slip and fall over into the abyss. Each bucket carried about five gallons and most of the time two or three of us would draw water using the four buckets we had at the house. The water was thick-tasting and pretty dirty. Often it contained grit and bugs that inhabited the well. But we drank the water and never got sick from it. Since water was scarce, bathing was a luxury. During the week, we would wash up in the wash pan with about a half gallon of water. Taking a bath was a once-a-week ritualistic activity so we would be fresh and clean for church on Sundays. A total body bath was an exercise in splurging or splashing that was supposed to last all week.

What we called the outhouse sat about fifty yards from the back door of the little house that Daddy built. This was the outdoor toilet. At night we used a chamber pot or slop jar if we needed it. Most of the time we would hold it until morning. The outdoor toilet was a big hole in the ground with a little two-by-four-foot house covering it. In later years, water also came from a well not too far from the outhouse. I'm not sure that waste water and drinking water weren't pretty much the same. They were no more than two hundred feet apart. There was no process of chlorination or filtration system to purify the water and kill bacteria. Still, it didn't kill us then and we're not dead yet. This is a miracle.

We used to do our homework by the dim light of the kerosene lamp. Most of the time this meant that when the sun went down, we went to bed. And we got up when the sun came up.

I always had a head cold or sinus infection that lasted most of the winter. Nose running or congested. Head-and stomachaches. No health insurance, which meant no doctor visits, unless you were sick unto death. The first time I went to the dentist, I was in the eleventh grade, sixteen years old. I wouldn't have gone then, if any of Daddy's concoctions had worked. Daddy was a jackleg in everything. He was both doctor and pharmacist, whose only credential was what he called "motherwit." The cavity was too large; the decay had gone to the nerve, the root. So, reluctantly, Daddy took me to see the dentist.

The dentist's office looked ominous and naturally smelled of disinfectant and medicine. Dr. Brooker, John S. Brooker DDS, had me sit in a large chair with lights hanging everywhere. I thought I was going to be electrocuted for the crime of having a toothache that Daddy could not fix. The chair could swivel and recline and do things that no other chair could do. With the touch of a switch, you could go from sitting tall and erect to lying flat on your back. One foot pedal raised you high in the air and another pedal placed you solidly in the grasp of the dentist's hands. It was the first time I had sat in a smart chair—a motorized, magic dental chair.

"Open your mouth wide. Wider now," the doctor bellowed as his hands began to probe my cuspids, bicuspids, molars, and wisdom teeth. He also checked for gum disease while he mangled my tongue as he pressed against my gums.

"Tell me where it hurts." I could barely speak because the pain was pulsating and the dentist's hands were prowling through my mouth. And yet I managed to respond.

"Right there, doctor. Right there," I managed to holler out while gasping for air.

"Looks like I'm going to have to take that tooth out. Uh, it's too decayed for a filling."

"Yes sir, uh, uh."

"Open wide now, so I can numb it up good." He was very good at talking to me and issuing directives, knowing that I couldn't respond because his fingers were fumbling around in my mouth.

As I opened my mouth, I saw the needle that looked like it was a foot long about to go into my gums. It was like a nightmare. I was scared almost unto death, though I pretended otherwise.

"Wider, open real wide, boy. This is just Novocain to keep you from feeling the pain. Let's give it a few minutes to work." It took an eternity to extract that tooth. Pulling and prying. Yanking and twisting. Then, suddenly, blood and saliva gushed forth from my mouth. And then I noticed the doctor place the blood-smeared tooth on a pan in front of me. I was relieved that the entire left side of my face was not in the pan. I felt as if the Doctor of Dental Surgery had cut my head off. I had no feeling at all on that side of my face.

"See, that's it. She was a large one. No more toothaches from this one." The doctor's large and stubby hands were covered with blood and spittle. He wore no prophylactic gloves and no protective face mask. Just a diamond ring and a gold watch. This was in 1968—long before dentists, physicians, and other health professionals were concerned about catching a disease from their patients or transmitting one. This was before root canals, crowns, implants, and gold fronts, or what the rappers call "grills," became vogue. I paid the dentist ten dollars that day and went on my swollen-mouth aching way.

We would sleep with three or four to a bed—often two at the head and two at the foot. We covered the thin blanket with coats and old rags to keep warm, because the winters were often quite frigid. Any joy of winter lay only in the knowledge that spring was around the corner, but I often felt that it took forever to arrive. I started thinking of spring the day after Christmas. Spring was greater than Christmas because it was a gift of warmth and sunshine. It was the promise and hope of God's long and sweet-smelling summer. I could hardly wait for springtime and summertime. No shoes needed. No coats or hats. No freezing from the wisp of the wind or the snow blowing in from the north. Summer was like the joy of heaven. It was a dream fulfilled every single year and I loved every minute of it.

What a joy to walk around in summertime with bare feet and scanty clothes. The years were 1958 through 1965 and I was so eager to start school. I couldn't wait to demonstrate my reading knowledge and my ability to comprehend words, sentences, and paragraphs. I could read and spell big words for as long as I can remember. Truthfully, I cannot remember a time when I could not read. This is not hubris or delusion; it is simply the truth as I remember it. Anything put before me: the English Bible, the newspaper, the dictionary, picture books, word books, the *Weekly Reader*, magazines, and, yes, the romance novels my oldest sister Marianna left on the couch. She was a romantic. Marianna was in love with a boy named Floyd Baker. In those days dating was a family affair where the whole family was present, by virtue of the house being so small. It was called "courting" back then. I remember Floyd asked Daddy about taking my sister out on a date. It seems so long ago and so old-fashioned.

"Mr. Harris, I'd like to take Marianna to the movies. Can I take her?"

"I don't see no reason for that. Ya'll don't need to be going to the movie alone."

"Mr. Harris, I . . . I'll have her back by nine o'clock."

"No, I don't think I can let you do that."

With those words, Marianna was doomed to a maiden life. An unhappy and confused life as an adult who used to live with my younger sister, Jackie. No husband and no children. Not the happiness or pleasure of Abraham or Sarah as seen in the Book of Genesis. But, it was more than that. Daddy was overprotective, and truthfully, my sister needed protecting because she was not very discerning and driven more by emotion than anything else. But, no one can always be protected by another. Not even Jim could always protect Huck. And Huck certainly could not protect Jim. And Daddy could not really protect my sister Marianna.

Chapter 9

I was born reading; I was gifted with the word. In his memoir *Father and Son*, Edmund Gosse's words about himself also applied to me: "I one day drew towards me a volume, and said, 'book' with startling distinctness. . . . I cannot recollect a time when a printed page of English was closed to me." Reading and writing were critical to understanding and excelling in school. I was good at both. So I was a young scholar throughout elementary school. Aside from the nightly visits to the Big House, we had no distractions. That's part of the reason I could excel in school. I loved school so much that I feel even now that I was born to go to school both as a learner and a teacher. Most of my life has been centered around school. Education is my passion.

In elementary school, I became the teacher's pet because I always wanted to please my teacher. My teachers were like goddesses. Gurus. Gandhi was indeed right in saying that true knowledge is impossible without a guru. They were all very attractive Black women. So, I think I was in love with my teachers as well as the opportunity to learn. I wanted to display good conduct and academic excellence. Whenever I was called upon to go to the blackboard to solve a math problem, spell a word, conjugate a verb, or write a sentence in cursive, I was eager to do it. I seldom missed a day of school. For years, I had perfect attendance. We never had to walk to school because, by the time I came along, we had public school buses, and since I had all Ss or Es (for satisfactory and excellent) in conduct and in all my other subjects, I got to be a school safety patrol. This meant that I sat on the front seat by the bus driver and would help to operate the school bus door and step outside to hold the safety patrol flag in front of the bus while all traffic came to a complete stop. Not that there was much traffic on the rural back roads where we lived and traveled. Nevertheless, I was happy to hold that coveted position.

My cousins used to horse around during the bus ride to school. They were a raucous bunch. William was accused of taking his "thang" out and showing it to a girl on the bus. There was a lot of laughter in the back of the bus that day. The bus driver pulled to the side of the road to investigate its cause.

"What's going on back here!" she screamed.

"He . . . he was trying to touch me with his private," the girl screamed.

"William, what was you doing back here, boy?"

"I wasn't doing nothing."

"Did you bother her?"

"My skin just touched her skin."

"I'm going to take you to the principal's office when we get to school. You come up here and sit beside your cousin James. You hear me, boy?"

"Yes ma'am, I hear you."

After William met with the principal and the investigation was complete (it only took a few minutes) he was expelled from school for five days. And, besides that, he had to sit in the front of the bus directly behind the driver for the rest of the school year. He was also admonished to keep his pants zipped up at all times. For years, we laughed and laughed at his explanation: "My skin just touched her skin."

Our first elementary school was about five miles from where we lived, and it was not much bigger than a large house. But it was still the biggest building I had ever entered. We could not attend the white children's school, which was less than one mile from our house—within walking distance. Every day, we passed the pretty red brick school with concrete sidewalks in front of it and large hedges and a manicured yard. The white folks' school was two or three stories high with a stone facade and a parapet wall spiraling above the slate roof. Balustrades. It had large Greek Revival columns. Oh, and lots and lots of floor-to-ceiling windows. It made education seem important and serious because the building spoke for itself. It was Jeffersonian. It looked like the ideal school, if there is such a thing. But for me and all the other Black children, it was not for us.

In stark contrast, just four miles away, was the Black children's school—Union Grove Elementary School. Windowpanes were broken. Bricks were missing from the steps. It sat off the main road on the edge of a soybean field and directly across from a cemetery. It was one level, brick exterior, paint peeling off the window frames, and the entire structure struggling to resemble a place where learning takes place, much less where it is a top priority. The contrast was glaring. And yet, we learned in spite of the ugly dilapidated building. We learned cultural anthropology and sociology. We learned the meaning of difference and the politics of segregation. This is described as savage inequality by Jonathan Kozol, the author of *Death at an Early Age*. Something was always wrong: leaking faucets, broken light fixtures, windowpanes missing, ceiling peeling, and roof leaking. I remember some cold days in the middle of January and February when there was no heat anywhere in the school. Was this Siberia or somewhere in Eastern Europe? Sometimes, it was so cold that we had to keep our coats on all day long. Those who had coats, that is. A coat in winter was a prized commodity because when you were one of ten poor children, as I was, simple economics taught that not everybody could get a coat. At least not one that fit perfectly or with buttons or a zipper that worked.

During one report card or grading period, the teacher wrote that I complained of headaches and stomachaches almost daily. "James is a good student, but he seems to suffer from constant headaches and stomachaches," she wrote. For the most part, I think I was simply congested and hungry. During those days it was hard for me to get enough to eat. I even looked malnourished. I was skinny as a bean pole.

My favorite teacher during this childhood period was an elegant, soft-spoken, and prim lady named Mrs. Gladys Oswald. She was so poised, so articulate, so polished. There was not a priggish bone in her body. I thought that the sun rose and set according to the will of Mrs. Oswald. She could write so elegantly. Every letter was perfectly placed within the lines and her cursive writing was flawless. I wanted one day to write like Mrs. Oswald. It was my dream. The Black teachers of that day apparently practiced writing every night when they went home. I certainly thought they did, because penmanship was a craft, an art. It was like Emily Dickinson's and Maya Angelou's poetry. Or the verse of Vascola Stoney and Adrienne Rich. It was photography, like the captivating shots of Marilyn Monroe's curvaceous, naked body by Milton H. Greene. It had its own narrative to it. It had a language that spoke of precision and respect. It said to the eyes, *Look at me. I have style and class; I am beautiful to behold.* It said to the hands, *I am curvaceous and slender and tall. Keep me within the lines. I am cursive.* Teachers were architects of the word. They were alphabet stylists. Calligraphers. And we were graded on how well we formed the letters to the alphabet. Style and substance are still one and the same. Writing well is not a bad thing, although any boy who did so was said to "write like a girl." This was reverse sexism. It's equivalent to saying that a Black student who studies hard and makes straight A's is "acting white." We've heard that craziness before. This is a foolish misinterpretation of

Black culture, Black pride, Black achievement, and the love of learning or learning for the sake of knowing; learning as a sign of intellectual curiosity; learning as a sense of pride. That's what it means to me. It means possessing good self-esteem. Lifelong learning is a virtue like prudence or honesty or truth or justice.

There was another very important and memorable thing about Mrs. Oswald, more important than her handwriting. She would often share her lunch with me—a half sandwich or some cheese crackers. Swiss, provolone, cheddar, American. Cheese from Vermont and Wisconsin. Imported cheeses from exotic places like Münster, Germany, and Paris, France. All types of cheeses. They all tasted mighty good to me. You see, I would, more often than not, eat my lunch while riding the bus to school because I was always hungry, and Mrs. Oswald felt sorry for me. Everyone knows that an apple butter sandwich will not last until lunchtime. It was made to be eaten before the lunch hour. Otherwise it would be a soggy mess.

It was a cold day in the month of March, right after Easter. Easter came early that year and it was our first day back to school after the holiday. Lunch time was the highlight of the school day. We had no cafeteria at that school, so everyone ate at their desks.

"Children, let's line up to wash our hands before we eat lunch."

"Mrs. Oswald, can I be first?"

"James, you were first yesterday. Let someone else go first today, OK?"

"Yes, ma'am." I waited my turn and then returned to my seat to stare at the ceiling while everybody around me ate their sandwiches. Mrs. Oswald couldn't help but notice that I had no lunch. I was sitting right in front of her, inhaling the smells of twenty or more lunches that taunted my aching taste buds. Peanut butter and jelly sandwiches. Ham and cheese. Bacon and egg sandwiches. I could smell the sweetness of apples and oranges. Cupcakes were dancing in my mouth. I was salivating like Ivan Pavlov's canines. Mrs. Oswald noticed. My head was down on the desk. I had no lunch. Just a six-ounce carton of milk. I was ashamed of being poor, but my poverty was not discomfiting enough to keep me from eating what was given to me.

"Boy, where is your lunch?" I shrugged my shoulders, embarrassed by the question. Mrs. Oswald inquired no further. She was too perceptive and smart to investigate further. Empathy and benevolence took hold of her, or was it Christian duty? Maybe, just good old common sense. She could sense my budding embarrassment about my own hunger.

"Here, try some of these Town House crackers with cheese. You might like half of my sandwich," she said quietly.

"Yes, ma'am. Thank you."

From that day forward, Mrs. Oswald included something for me when she prepared her lunch. It didn't fill me up, but it abated my hunger. I was her lunch buddy for the rest of the year. I was the beneficiary of her kindness and empathy.

My own lunch was usually an apple butter sandwich or a peanut butter and jelly sandwich or sometimes it was a biscuit with a slice of fried fatback in the middle. Whenever I could pilfer enough pennies from the kitchen floor or the pockets of Daddy's pants, I would buy chocolate milk at the school for a nickel. I loved chocolate milk; no, I craved chocolate milk. It was like a stimulant for me. It was an energy booster. A liquid pill in a box. Regular Grade A, homogenized, pasteurized whole milk was not as tasty, and whenever I was given a choice, I always chose chocolate. The deep dark smooth color of African people. Beautiful, tasteful, choc-o-late. It was probably the abundance of sugar in the chocolate syrup that gave it such a taste.

The school building we were housed in—as rickety and ragged as it was—was not as bad as the school books. They were the discarded, the discontinued, the old editions of every subject. They were ragged and worn, marked up and vandalized on purpose. Some of the books had pages missing and backs torn off. White children from years past had used these books until they were deemed discards; then they would be carted off to the Black schools for us to use. Not that there was anything salvific about freedom and justice in the books either. Another example of the blatant inequality of segregation. The books were always used and splattered with bad words. Profanity. Ugly words: *niggers, spooks, coons, monkeys.* Pictures of Blacks would be embellished: teeth blackened, ears and lips enlarged like they'd been injected with Botox. The books looked like they had been edited by Mark Twain's illustrator E. W. Kemble, who was a master of the caricature of Blacks.

Darker-skinned children were treated with less favor than light-skinned Blacks by teachers, school administrators, and children themselves. It was hard for dark-complexioned children to do well in school. There was a color caste and class system within the Black classroom. Educated Blacks, or as Carter G. Woodson said, "mis-educated Negroes," had begun to hate themselves to the extent that "white was right, Black get back, brown stick around" was the modus operandi. Black teachers had internalized the ways of their colonizers. The darker you were, the less favor you received. Lighter-skinned children were presumed to be smarter by Black teachers. Colorism is real. This was a fallacy that my dark-skinned body proved every day I sat in the classroom. I was always in the top group for reading, spelling, and math. Ability grouping or tracking meant nothing to me. I was always in group one because there was no word that I couldn't pronounce and no word I couldn't spell. James Henry could read. Big words, too!

Colorism be damned. As the young brother in my church would say, "That's dead."

I looked up to the school principal. He had authority and power. Maybe because he wore a necktie and a starched white shirt every day. He fit the description of Twain's "nigger" professor. One day he came to our classroom and asked the teacher to allow me to ride with him to the school board office, since I was deemed a model student. I was excited. I got to ride in the principal's shiny new Chevrolet. I was riding with "Mr. Big-shot." The man. Our principal was a cigar-and-cigarette smoking, fast-driving, slick-headed man who ruled the school with an iron fist. To me, he acted very much like a slave master or an overseer who kept all the female teachers standing in subjection and fear. He was the only male in the school's leadership and faculty. Black patriarchy was mimicking white authority. The janitor, however, was a Black man, too, but he was voiceless and powerless. A peon. He was of a lower socioeconomic and educational class. There was no respect for him by the principal or most of the teachers. He did all the dirty work: cleaned toilets, mopped floors, collected trash, washed the blackboards, cut the grass. You name it and he did it. But he had something else going for himself because we knew a secret that the bourgeois principal didn't know.

We were riding the bus home and when we got off together, my cousin Wilber said to me, "I know a secret. Something you don't know. Nobody knows this but me. Guess what?"

"Come on. What?"

"I saw Mr. Johnson huggin' and smooching Ms. Williams over by the water fountain—in the little supply room at the end of the hall. It looked like they were having sex. When they saw me, they pretended to be just talkin.' She jumped away."

"What? Are you sure you ain't making this stuff up?" I said.

"No, man. This ain't the first time I seen 'em doing it. About a week ago, I saw 'em tryin' to 'do it' when everybody was outside for recess. My teacher had sent me back in the building to get my coat 'cause it was cold outside. When I passed the little room, they was kissin' and stuff. I acted like I didn't see nothin."

"Well, how do I know you ain't lying? You lyin' 'cause you always lie."

"I know it's true 'cause Ms. Williams gave me a quarter yesterday and told me to get an ice cream to go with my lunch. I ain't ask her for it neither. She been all nice to me for a reason."

"That don't mean nothing."

"Yes it do 'cause I get ice cream every day now. Every since I seen what I seen."

Wow! Imagine that. The janitor was doing more than mopping floors and cleaning windows. And I learned how to keep a secret, though I was tempted to try to get me some ice cream too. But, to do that, I would have to snitch on my cousin. And I couldn't bring myself to do that. So I kept my mouth shut. I never said a word—until now.

Black leaders are often chosen because of their ability to keep other Blacks under control and in subjection. Black educators have always been status quo–oriented, perpetuating an ideology that is more conformist than anything else. Education for freedom and liberation has not been uppermost in their pedagogy or in their lesson plans. Education for placation is the norm. Education for becoming a part of the system or education for consolation seems to be more like it. "Don't rock the boat that you are riding on" is the prevailing philosophy for those teaching in the public schools of urban America. It was the case then and seems to still be the case today. Education and the miseducation of the Negro. This is something to think about as we ponder public policies regarding standards of learning and No Child Left Behind. Children are being left behind by the thousands and everybody knows it. Everybody is sworn to secrecy and pretending all is well. They are pretending they don't know the truth, as if they're waiting to receive ice cream sandwiches the way my cousin was. And, in the meantime, our Black children cannot read. I see the vestiges of this in college and seminary students. Yes, most of them have diplomas and degrees, but as Du Bois suggested, the Black college has to do a lot of remedial work with students who have been neglected and deprived of a strong reading and math-based education from pre-K through twelfth grade.

Chapter 10

I imagine if I had read *Adventures of Huckleberry Finn* in high school, my life would have been different. My perspective on Twain and the whole cast of characters could have benefitted from a teacher capable of explaining some of the offensive language and broad themes in the book: race and the language of racism, American aristocracy, a culture of fraud, gender differences, and the belief that people are like sheep who need to be controlled. Alas, high school had nothing to do with Mark Twain for me.

When the seminar gathered for the sixth or seventh week, I realized that Garth, who had the tattoo of the Confederate flag on his arm, the man I noticed on the first day but didn't yet know his name or anything else about him, was in fact a high school English teacher. He taught *Adventures of Huckleberry Finn* to ninth and tenth graders at Robert E. Lee School in Henrico County. I asked him about his personal feelings regarding Twain's use of *nigger* in the book and how he approached it as a teacher. He gave me a lecture on America and the South in the 1840s and 1850s and said, "Mark Twain was simply speaking the language of the masses. Everybody in America referred to Blacks as *niggers* during that period. It was common practice."

I said politely, "Thank you for that, but how do you explain to your class that there is a certain bias and racism inherent in the etiology of the word?"

"I, I, I try to make a distinction between then and now," he said. I noticed that he was getting upset with my questions, so I quit. But before I stopped, I asked one final question.

"Garth, do you have any Black kids in your class, and if so how do they respond to the word when their white counterparts use it?"

"No, I've been teaching the course now for five years and not a single Black student has enrolled in the class. It is an Advanced Placement or AP English class and only those with a certain grade point average qualify to get in."

"What are you saying? That in your school, there are no Black students qualified to take your course?"

"No, no, I'm saying that I don't know what the problem is."

"Well, I think I have an idea of the problem. Have you personally tried to recruit Blacks for the class?" The discussion ended without any agreement and I began to realize that I was not making a lot of friends in that class. So I quit talking for the day.

When it was time for me to go to high school I was nervous and afraid. It was a new experience because none of my four older siblings had made it that far. It was the biggest school I had ever set foot in. And with all the students in the gym, in the hallway, and in the classrooms, it seemed like thousands. Every Black high school student in Chesterfield County went to Carver because it was the only high school there for Blacks in 1965. Segregation was the custom in spite of the law. From Ettrick-Matoaca to Forrest Hill to Midlothian to Winterpock, every Black hamlet fed into Carver High, where the principal and all the teachers were as Black as the students. All except one. The art teacher was a white woman with red hair and lots of freckles to match. She was a brave soul, as artists often are.

The first day was an eye-opener for me. A revelation. These students looked like adults, and everybody appeared bigger than I was. I felt like a fish out of water. It was the only day in my life that I was unable to eat my lunch. My cousins Carolyn, Alma, and Charles were astonished at my loss of appetite. They reasoned that I had to be sick. And indeed, I was sick to my stomach by the overwhelming size of the school and the large number of students. Strangers. For seven years I had sat in the same small classroom with one teacher and now without any orientation or preparation, I had six classes—each lasting only one hour. I was experiencing culture shock.

There were only eight or ten males in the college-prep track: Brandon, Michael, Theophilus, Anthony, Reginald, Thomas, Earl, Nathaniel, Floyd, and me. I believe there was one other guy whose name escapes me, but I can remember his awkward personality and clumsy behavior. High school was a rite of passage. It was part of the drama from childhood to youth to adulthood. I learned to cuss proudly in high school. I imagine that as budding adolescents driven by puberty's hold on our eager and receptive bodies, pulling us inch by inch and a few pubic hairs at a time into this new realm of manhood and womanhood—adulthood—the tendency and desire to cuss, lie, and steal from the corner store was indeed a part of the maturation process. It was the semiotics of youthful bliss, embracing a careless and carefree attitude and behavior. Words and phrases that I had never heard in our *communio sanctorum* of a house became a part of the new high school vocabulary. I had never ever heard my mother or father use a cuss word—not that I knew for sure that they didn't cuss every now and then—but high school was a different culture. It was a lying and cussing subculture. In addition to Spanish and French, cussing was the unofficial new language for me. Profanity was cool. It was a part of the social studies curriculum. My new friends were all talking this way: "Kiss my ass," "Damn this and that," "Hell no," "Bullshit," "Bitch-ass," and so on. And, we had never read J. D. Salinger's *The Catcher in the Rye* where Holden Caulfield's signature *goddamn* permeates the book just like the word *nigger* is plastered on the pages of *Adventures of Huckleberry Finn*.

My cousins Carmen and Maryellen taught me that girls could cuss just as much as boys. They were talking about a boy whom Carmen had a crush on. The boy, Donald Tutwiler, was pursuing several girls at the same time. I overheard my cousins as they walked along the hall fuming about their social and sexual dissatisfaction.

"I'm gonna kick her ass," Carmen said.

"That bitch don't know who she's messing with," Maryellen egged her on.

"You let me catch that heifer by herself. I'm gonna give her a piece of my mind."

As eighth and ninth graders in Carver High School, we were determined to express our growth and development in a language that was borderline profane and yet felt so cool. Scatological humor was in the air. Language that suggested we were grown. Masculine. We were boys being drawn into manhood. We could say whatever we wanted to say and we could do as we pleased. UC Berkley had influenced us because free speech was in the air we breathed and in the water we drank. With hormones in large supply, we could go from flaccidity to priapism in a few seconds without any visible female provocation. Just a thought or a daydream about a girl could bring on an unwanted and embarrassing erection. At that age, wet dreams and romance were hormonal equals. Sex was in the air. It was everywhere. Unlike Marvin Gaye's anthem *What's Going On?*, we knew what was going on. Or so we thought. Piety and ignorance are often one and the same. But not always.

In high school, I wanted to be like everyone else. Desperately. Naturally. I wanted to fit in and to be liked by others in my class and in the school. It's hard to believe, but in retrospect, I was like Huckleberry Finn, who always wanted to be like Tom Sawyer. Why is it that I always wanted to be like somebody else? The answer lies in human nature. All of us want to be liked and accepted by others no matter how often we say otherwise. Self-deception is a part of human nature. And, the greatest liar is the one I see in the mirror every time I wash my face.

Peer pressure was upon me. So, yes, gradually, I too learned to cuss with a "matter of fact" posture by emulating my classmates. Thank God I didn't join "a band of Robbers" like Huck did. I mimicked my more popular classmates though it did not come naturally to me. I was not a natural-born cusser. I was a *faux* cusser. I was more like an intern in the art of cussing. It took too much effort for me to fit in. As a matter of fact, it was really out of character for me, but I couldn't let on. The truth is that I didn't feel right cussing, but I also believe that I tried to do what my friends were doing. That was the motivating factor. It is a scary fact as I think about it now. But I never called another Black student, or classmate, a nigger because that word was considered on par with using God's name in vain. I'm still not convinced that the forbidden word should have a place in popular culture. As a matter of fact, during the first three years of high school, we were still Negroes. Not yet Black. Stokely Carmichael had not yet used the term *Black Power* in Greenwood, Mississippi. And James Brown, the godfather of soul music, had not yet recorded "Say It Loud, I'm Black and I'm Proud." We would never dare call each other "nigger," not as Jim does in *Adventures of Huckleberry Finn*. And not as young Blacks do today; Nigga.

I also tried smoking cigarettes because my friends did it. I think now of Huck, although I never felt the way he felt, that smoking was a moral good on par with truth and love.

Huck was wrong and I was wrong. There is no good in smoking. Lung cancer, heart disease, high blood pressure, and asthma have proven that smoking is more deadly than cool. The tobacco companies lied, and, we all believed they were telling the truth. We believed what we wanted to believe. It's easier that way.

There was no hard drug use in our school; I always knew that over time, the use of hard drugs was the kiss of death. And, to the best of my knowledge, none of my high school friends did drugs, but some of my cousins did. Most of them are dead now. Some say that drugs played a role in my older sister's death. I don't know for sure, but I know obesity, high blood pressure, depression, and smoking cigarettes played a big role. There were drugs in the high school, though. Sometimes you could smell the stench of marijuana behind the school or in the back hallway. It can be a prelude to the more dangerous stuff, a gateway drug, so they say, and I believe it. That's why, to this day, I have never smoked weed.

I did get my first taste of Bacardi rum from a classmate whose nickname was "Red" because he and his sister were the fairest-looking students in the entire school. At the time, he looked white to me. "Harris, look what I got, man." The liquid was a bit golden in color. Looked like urine or kerosene oil to me. I felt the pint bottle. He opened it and the intoxicating sweet aroma crawled up my nose like it was Aramis or Old Spice. Acting as if I knew what I was doing, I began to lift the bottle to my mouth and drink to be worldly; I was willing to try anything in a desire to overcome my backwater adolescent ignorance and to fit in with the urban social culture of those in my class.

"Man, go 'head and take a swig."

"OK. I'll give it a try," I said. I took a big gulp and felt as if my mouth, throat, and stomach were on fire. I was choking on high octane alcohol fumes. I didn't let on, but I thought it was pretty nasty. It was way too strong for a weaklin' like me. I didn't want to be a wimp, though. Red wiped the top with his hand and took another gulp. And just as he was handing the bottle back to me, the school bell rang. It was time for class to start. I had been saved by the bell—not totally though. That one drink made me wobbly and a bit too drowsy and depressingly dull for the rest of the day. I was too friendly and bold—using cuss words without fear like Holden Caulfield's "goddamn phonies" in *The Catcher in the Rye*.

Another crazy thing happened during the same year of high school that was really dangerous and wild. We were lucky, though. My daddy used to say, "God protects babies and fools." The Bible, too, speaks of fools. And we were quite foolish. The wisdom of the book of Proverbs applied to us, literally. Read the Proverbs of Solomon, son of David, King of Israel:

> Like snow in summer or rain in harvest, so honor is not fitting for a fool. . . . Do not answer fools according to their folly, or you will be a fool yourself. . . . Do you see persons wise in their own eyes? There is more hope for fools than for them.

One of my foolish classmates brought a gun to chemistry class one day. A .38 caliber pistol. It was crazy. He was a fool. It's a miracle nobody got shot and killed that day, but in the language of Huck "we was awful afraid." I don't know if our teacher, Mr. James Pretlow, ever knew what was happening. While he was teaching us how to preserve a frog in formaldehyde or to understand the periodic table of elements, there was a subculture of violence and juvenile delinquency trying to raise its ugly head right there in our chemistry class. Earl Boswell was a little short guy who had a beef with somebody. I think it was a boy named Michael Cunningham. So he brought a gun to intimidate, threaten, and possibly shoot Michael and anyone who got in the way. This was long before violence made its way to rural Chesterfield County Public schools. I don't remember exactly what happened that day except somebody spotted the gun and yelled, "He's got a gun." Pandemonium broke out. The entire class went scrambling for the door. Chemistry lessons and experiments be damned. Self-preservation always trumps knowledge no matter how ignorant or unwise that preserved self or forbidden knowledge may be. I made my way to safety that day and the gun was never fired. Earl was suspended for a day or so and came back to school as if nothing ever happened. Those were the good 'ole days before the tragedies of Columbine and Virginia Tech and Northern Illinois. It was before Kent State. I think 1968 was a turning point in American idealism. It was a violent year. And we will never really know how many people died in the Vietnam War during that same year. But we do know that Martin Luther King Jr. and Bobby Kennedy were assassinated during that awful year—1968.

But at the time we were too busy trying to impress the teachers, the females, and each other to stray too far off the beaten path. I didn't have many close friends then and I don't have many now. And, if the truth be told, I don't want any more than I have. Friends are too much like peeling onions. They make you cry. Not just friends, but family also. The fewer, the better when it comes to sorrow. This often saves a lot of pain and agony—and money. My family is large and needy, so I believe I know what I'm talking about.

During this same school year, my younger brother, Douglas, took sick. Really sick. I was just two years older than Doug, but you would've thought that I was old enough to be his father. Daddy and Momma put a lot on my shoulders: buying groceries every week, visiting the schools, taking siblings to the doctor, and filling out papers of any kind.

I took my brother to the doctor that day. As usual, Daddy went to work in the woods cutting and hauling pulpwood. Mother stayed home with the rest of the children. Doug had been sick all weekend long and complained of a severe headache when he was not asleep. He could not stay awake for long without slipping into a sonorous slumber. Sleeping day and night. Weak. Running a high fever. Body aches. Unable to eat. Nobody in our family had ever been that sick before. I was scared. So, in fear and trembling, I took him to see Dr. Calvin Thigpen, a brilliant and compassionate general practice physician. He was full of compassion and kindness. He was a man of wisdom. A doctor.

While waiting in the doctor's office on the second floor of the building on South Avenue in Petersburg, my brother collapsed—dropping to the floor like a rag doll. We had only been there a few minutes crouched among a room full of sick people. He was weak and exhausted from walking across the street and up the flight of stairs. As he fell to the floor, he began to convulse with a seizure. Old men and women waiting to see the doctor began to scoot their chairs to the side of the wall. They, too, were in a panic. A lot of commotion ensued. While I was nervous on the inside, my outward demeanor was calm and collected. But, it was no more than a grand facade.

"Dr. Thigpen, you need to come out here quick," the receptionist yelled.

The doctor was in the back room with another patient.

"Oh my God, what's wrong with him?" asked another patient waiting to see the doctor.

I was leaning over my younger brother in a state of helplessness and shock as Dr. Thigpen, a stout, dark-brown-skinned, graying man in his mid-forties, began to insert a wooden depressor in Doug's mouth to keep him from choking or swallowing his tongue. Doug's body was shaking. Spasms engulfed him and he was out of control. He was heaving and sweating profusely. His eyes rolled back into his head. The doctor pulled out a syringe and gave him a shot of epinephrine to minimize the impact of the seizure. Dr. Thigpen was cool, calm, and collected as he instructed his nurse: "Call the emergency operator. Get an ambulance over here. Tell 'em to come upstairs to my office. The second floor, 201 South Avenue."

"Yes sir, doctor."

Doctor Thigpen worked on my brother until the ambulance arrived. The paramedics checked his pulse, unbuttoned his shirt, and placed a pillow under his head; they were at the office in less than ten minutes, although it seemed like an eternity to me. I knew Doug must have been gravely ill because the doctor didn't want him taken to the local ER at Petersburg General Hospital—less than a mile from his office. Instead, he wanted him transported to the Medical College of Virginia, a trauma center and the most prominent teaching and research hospital in the entire state. The doctor's voice was raised, yet calm. I was interpreting every word. Every gesture. The intonation, the sound of urgency permeating the doctor's behavior as he told the paramedics to transport Doug to the hospital ER in Richmond. He was unfazed by all the rancor and disarray in his office.

"I want him taken to the Medical College of Virginia and I want you to give the emergency room doctor these notes." I thought I saw him write the word *epilepsy* or *episodic* seizures on the prescription pad he handed to the paramedic.

"Yes sir, doctor. We'll get him there as soon as possible."

"Make it quick, OK?" The paramedic nodded his head in agreement but didn't say a word.

The doctor kept scribbling his thoughts on a prescription pad as the paramedics placed my brother on the stretcher. I was fifteen years old and Douglas was only thirteen. I was overtaken by fear that day, but there was no time to show it. I had to help my brother and I had to do what Daddy asked me to do. Anything for Daddy because Daddy was our rock. And anything for Douglas, my younger brother.

I wondered, why would a medical doctor call the ambulance? Why couldn't he do something more than just palliate my brother? I was afraid that my brother was going to die between Dr. Thigpen's office and the ER at MCV. After all the

commotion, I got into the front passenger seat beside the driver
and we raced up Interstate 95 from Petersburg to Richmond,
which is about twenty-five miles north of Petersburg. I don't
think I had ever been to Richmond before that day. Certainly
not at that speed. Siren and horn blowing. Red lights flashing.
We passed everybody. Cars pulled to the right lane to let us
zoom by. I prayed that God would take care of my brother. I
was scared, but I was glad that we hadn't waited any longer
to take him to the doctor. As a rule, we didn't go to the doctor unless it was the only alternative. Daddy would otherwise
concoct his own medicine from the leaves and roots of plants
and trees behind the house. He would always warn me: "James
Henry, don't you ever try this 'cause it can kill you if you don't
know what you're doing."

"Yes sir," was my only response. I had no intention of cooking up my own hemlock. I didn't know one leaf from the other.
One root from the next. I was curious, but not that curious. I
had heard the idiom "curiosity killed the cat." I was young and
stupid, but I was not *that* stupid.

We had no medical or health insurance and were too proud
to accept Medicaid or any public assistance. Mother and Daddy
would concoct home remedies and feed us castor oil and syrup of
Black-Draught and rub us in camphorated oil as the antidote to
sickness. B.C. powder and Bayer aspirin were standard for headaches and most other aches. This was before Tylenol, Aleve, and
other over-the-counter remedies. This normally took care of the
situation, but when Doug did not get better after all these potions
had been given him, Daddy told me, "James Henry, I want you to
take your brother to the doctor in the morning. First thing. Take
this ten dollars for the doctor." Ten dollars covered everything!

"Yes sir. I'll try to get James Booker to give us a ride." And, it
wasn't a minute too soon. We got up early to get ready. Mother
had to dress Doug, because he was so frail and weak from not

eating for nearly three days. Maybe he'd had a cup of soup. If Doug had had a seizure at home it would have taken an hour for the paramedics to get to where we lived. He could have choked to death by the time they got there.

We arrived in Richmond in what seemed like a few minutes. This is the state capital, with skyscrapers and restaurants everywhere. The first restaurant I saw near the sprawling hospital was a place where doctors and nurses hung out. For me it had the most morbid and frightening name: Skull and Bones. I thought it was a bad joke. A name like that around the corner from the hospital's emergency room and morgue, and a short distance from the state medical examiner's office! This was too real for me—especially since my brother had a severe headache and a temperature above 102 degrees and was having episodic seizures.

The doctors and nurses kept my brother in the ER all day and half the night. I saw men and women in short and long white coats coming and going. Medical students, interns, chaplains, resident physicians, and the acclaimed doctors who were on the teaching faculty. Doctors from Asia, the Middle East, Africa, Latin America, and the United States were looking in his eyes, ears, nose, and throat. They were feeling his pulse, checking his heart, oxygen level, and so many things I knew nothing about. I heard one doctor say to the nurse on duty, "Let's order an EKG, CBC, and EEG. And get me a neurologist down here stat." The word "stat" caused me to tremble with fear.

"What about an X-ray of his skull? I need to see what's happening around his brain." I thought *neurological disorder*. I knew a few terms like *cerebellum*, *medulla oblongata*, and *thalamus*. My mind was racing with the little knowledge of anatomy and medicine I had gained from reading the World Book Encyclopedia. A little knowledge is a dangerous and insecure thing.

"Also, get this boy out of here so we can get the sick one into a bed in the neurology ICU. Is there a parent or guardian with this child? Anybody other than his brother? We have two children here," the doctor mumbled.

"My dad is at work and my mother is home with my brothers and sisters. I'm the only one here with my brother," I said. "I'm responsible for him."

"Somebody needs to sign these forms in case we have to operate on him today."

"I'll sign. He's my brother. I'll sign them." I was scared to death. What was I signing for? What would they do to him? I thought, *Experiment. Medical research.* I had heard stories of what these doctors were capable of. My imagination combined with fear and ignorance almost caused me to faint. But I didn't. My brother stayed in the hospital for nearly two weeks. At first, it was touch and go, but as the days went by, he began to stabilize and so he escaped brain surgery. I learned later that he had contracted a viral infection that was very rare in these parts. The doctor called it viral encephalitis, an inflammation of the area around his brain. During this entire period, he was alert and talkative, although he lost a lot of weight from being in the hospital on a bland liquid diet.

My twin cousins Timothy and Tony were a godsend. They visited Doug in the hospital and drove us back and forth to Richmond each time Doug had to go back to the neurology clinic to see the doctors. This went on for a year or more, but Doug fully recovered. He never had another seizure. No more severe headaches. Praise God from whom all blessings flow.

However, for years, I could not watch any emergency medical program on TV and I became fearful of hospitals and doctors. And, even today, doctors make me nervous and cause my blood pressure to rise and my pulse rate to increase. It takes a good while for me to calm down whenever I go to visit the doctor. It's the white coat and the stethoscope that cause me to overreact with fear and trembling.

Chapter 11

Petersburg is a depressed old-style little town, but during the time I was growing up, it was booming. The economy was driven by the golden leaf of flue-cured tobacco. It didn't take long for the word to spread on South Avenue that Douglas had gotten sick in the doctor's office and that he had to be transported to Richmond's famed Medical College of Virginia. On the Avenue things were bustling. My Uncle Thomas ran a barber shop on the first floor and my Aunt Josephine ran a beauty shop just a few doors down on the second floor in the same building as Dr. Thigpen's office. The barber shop was like a saloon of the old West, and I had the suspicion that you could get more than your hair trimmed or a shave. The barber shop was a social club. It was a place to relax and to get a drink by the shot or play the numbers. There was a back room where people—strange-looking men and women—were always coming and going. Any time of day or night I went there, I noticed some folk stumbling and staggering, others laughing, still others came in the front door and walked straight to the back room without saying a word. The barber shop was like a storefront church—full of hoopla and excitement. It was a spectacle where getting a haircut was a sociocultural event.

My cousin Geraldine worked as a receptionist in the doctor's office. So the word about Doug's illness spread like wildfire. The truth is that I was no stranger to the ER because one summer I was playing around with the washing machine at Aunt Emma's house and got my fingers caught in the wringer affixed to the top of the washing machine. Blood spewed everywhere as my index finger was crushed and split from the rest of my hand, dangling like a broken limb from a sycamore tree. My aunt and several of my cousins heard me holler and immediately recognized that I needed to go to the doctor. To the hospital. This was an emergency. Aunt Emma gathered her things and asked James Booker, our surrogate cousin, handyman, and designated driver, to hurry us to Petersburg General Hospital. None of my aunts had a driver's license, and I don't remember any of my uncles ever trying to teach them to drive. This was the practice of Black patriarchy. Women's suffering was everywhere.

I can still feel the bright lights shining down on me as I lay on the hospital examination table. I can hear the doctor's voice: "Young man, can you move your index finger?"

"I'll try," I said as my finger was dangling lifelessly from my hand.

"Well, if you can't move it, all the nerves must be dead. I'll have to amputate it—to cut it off," he said.

"No! I believe I can move it, doctor." The doctor's question and response were more than alarming. I could take the pain of stitches better than I could his brusque bedside manners. I thought he was a brute. A butcher in a doctor's white coat. The real Dr. Jekyll. What kind of doctor tells a child that he has to cut his finger off?

Like a flash of lightning, I moved my finger and with alacrity began to move my entire hand. I thought that the doctor was crazy to suggest amputating my finger. This real-world Dr. Jekyll scared me out of my wits! Never again would I stick my hand in such a contraption as the wringer of an old washing machine. My electrical and mechanical engineering curiosity died on the crazy doctor's examination table that very day.

I had another Petersburg General Hospital experience. The year before my brother Douglas got sick, my cousin and I were chopping wood for the stove just about two yards from the house at the edge of the woods. My cousin's name was Ernest, but we called him by his middle name, Willie. I held the wood while Willie chopped with the ax. Somehow when he swung the ax back to cut the wood, it hit me in the head and cut a six- to eight-inch gash through my eyebrow above my left eye. I ran to the house screaming, holding my head. My mother thought I had been cut in the eye. She let out a blood-curdling scream as soon as she saw my face, hands, and shirt covered in blood.

"Richard, James Henry has been cut with an ax," she screamed as Daddy came running.

"Let me see your face, boy." I was holding my forehead, covering my left eye. Daddy and Mother quickly assessed the damage and called for Uncle C. F. to take me to the hospital. I remember Uncle C. F., Daddy, and Momma, all three of them washing the blood from my face and hands and putting me in some clean clothes and Daddy and Uncle C. F. racing me down the road across the bridge and the railroad tracks to the hospital's emergency room.

"How you feel, son?" Daddy and Uncle C. F. asked. I was equally at home with both of them. I had two fathers. More than that, really. These two guys were partners in raising all of us.

"I think I'm OK. My head hurts real bad, though."

At the hospital, Dr. Johnson said that I had a concussion from the blow of the ax. According to the X-ray I had no skull or brain damage. I remember being in the operating room that time. Lights, lots of lights, and nurses all around me. The doctor kept talking to me in an effort to assess the damage to my head. He gave me a shot of something to help ease the pain and ward off infection while he stitched me up. No CT scans or MRIs were available back then. Just the doctor's wisdom, scientific knowledge, and medical skills. Clinical experience too.

"Can you see my fingers?" the doctor asked.

"Yes sir."

"How many?"

"Two," I said. Or was it one? I prayed that I had no double vision.

"OK. You'll be as good as new in about a week." But he still wasn't quite sure.

"Tell me your name, son. Do you know your full name?"

"James Henry Harris."

"What grade are you in? In what school?"

"Fifth grade. Dupuy Elementary School."

"How old are you? Do you know your age? When were you born?"

"I am eleven years old. I was born on June 3, 1952," I said.

"Good. That's good."

The doctor sewed me up after this cascade of correctly answered questions. Twenty-some stitches in my forehead just centimeters from my left eye.

"You're a lucky boy and you will be OK. There will be some swelling of your face in the next twenty-four hours. Just tell your mother to help you keep an ice compress on it. And take the medicine I'm giving you. Come back to my office in five days so I can put on new bandages."

He was talking to me and Daddy at the same time. Daddy was more nervous than I was. He knew that I could have been killed, maimed, or blinded for life if the cut had been one or two centimeters in any other direction. This was the grace of God at work in my life. Daddy was also nervous by nature. The smallest thing would set him off pacing the floor and smoking cigarettes. He had a restive spirit—driven by love, anxiety, or fear. Or something else that I never knew about. Maybe it was childhood experience, or it could have simply been his nature. He worried about everything. My aunts said that when my grandmother (their mother) was pregnant with Daddy she had been in an accident. While riding in a horse-drawn wagon something scared the horse and the wagon flipped over, throwing my grandmother out. They said it was a ghost, because horses can see the wind or spirits, and that this affected Daddy, the unborn child. While this story explains some of Daddy's nervousness, I don't know whether it's truth or a myth. All I know for sure is that Daddy was easily agitated. He was worried about everything, even the things he could not change. And, I know that over time, myths turn into beliefs and truth for most people.

I never once heard my father use a cuss word the whole time we were growing up. Not once. No matter how mad or upset he got. He did a few other memorable things, though. He got so angry once that he ran all of us out of the house into a small shed in the backyard. It was in the midst of a summer thunderstorm. Lightning flashing, thunder rolling through the wind-swept rain made the day feel like the dawn of Armageddon. Something had pissed him off mighty bad. I don't know what it was about, but I know he was very angry and out of control. He was like a raging bull that particular day. So my mother gathered us up and scurried out the back door. My daddy's temper was sharp but fleeting. After a while, we all went back into the house. The storm was over. His temper tantrum and all.

There were many times when we had to sit in silence because Daddy also suffered from severe migraine headaches, which were probably exacerbated by clogged sinuses. He was always blowing his nose or clearing his throat of nasal drip. The headaches were aggravated by smoking cigarettes and taking BC Powder chased with a Pepsi Cola as a remedy.

My cousins used to mimic and mock Daddy's efforts to clear his head and throat of mucus and phlegm. Children are often mean and insensitive to one another, at least for a moment.

Within minutes they forget their taunts and move on to something else after swearing not to do it again. In a sense, as children, we are all like Huckleberry Finn: self-righteous tricksters, pranksters. We treat each other the way Huck often treated Jim. The only difference is that Huck was twelve years old and Jim was a grown man with two children of his own. Yet, the man-child Huck thought of Jim as a child and treated him as such. This was because a white child was assumed to be totally superior to an adult male slave. Huck often treated Jim like a slave, too—even a nigger because niggers and slaves were all the same.

My mother seldom raised her voice. She was a quiet, calm spirit. Beautiful. I think about the fact that she always had children pulling on her. We were like a litter of critters. As soon as one child was weaned off breast milk, my mother's stomach was protruding again. There was no talk of sex and very little obvious expression of sexuality. Mothers are not sexual objects. They are angels from heaven. But, you can imagine that in a small, two-room house the sounds of sex could not be hidden by the cloak of night. It had to be quick and subdued—I, for one, was a light sleeper. I could hear the crickets, the frogs, the birds, and the owls all making their fertile, nocturnal noises. I could hear my mother and daddy go at it when they thought we all were deep in the fog of sleep. When I first heard it and put "two and two" together, I was afraid of the truth. I was trying not to listen and wished I was asleep. In the small hours of the morning, I could hear the restrained grunts and gasps of pleasure and pain as my parents made love. I came to calculate that around nine months later, there would be born another baby. And so it was. Like clockwork. Like the phases of the moon or the surety of the sunrise.

I had just finished high school during the summer that my youngest sister, Jackie, was born, the first day of August 1970.

She was my mother's eleventh child, born eighteen years after me and twenty-eight years after my oldest sister. My mother was pregnant for nearly thirty consecutive years. They did not believe in birth control: no pills, no condoms, no vasectomy, and no tubal ligation. Just unprotected and natural sex, like the birds and the bees. During the last pregnancy, Mother was considered beyond the age of childbearing. She was forty-five years old and my daddy was fifty. No menopause allowed and no Viagra needed. Carrie Anna and Richard were like Sarah and Abraham in the Bible except there was no prediction and no laughter about the impossible.

Even in my youthful ignorance, I felt that this was a difficult pregnancy for my mother. Her ankles and legs would swell because of fluid retention and during the hot and humid months of June, July, and August she could barely move around. We had no air conditioning. These were the dog days of summer, in more than one way. For her and for the rest of us, misery was written all over our faces. My brother and I would take turns massaging our mother's legs and ankles with wintergreen rubbing alcohol and warm towels soaked in the aseptic solution of Epsom salt and warm water, in an effort to reduce the pain and swelling and make her feel better.

You can imagine that my mother was not able to attend my high school graduation that year because she was too busy struggling to maintain her own health while trying to carry my soon-to-be baby sister to full term. In addition to the fluid build-up in her feet, ankles, and legs, she also had high blood pressure and probably some other problems that I didn't know about. I had always been inquisitive. But I didn't ask any questions when the doctor placed Momma on more bed rest and told her to keep her legs elevated for a certain length of time each day. I knew this was hard on her body and mind because it was hard on me and the rest of us. And I reasoned, in this case, that the less I knew, the better. I was the one who had calculated earlier that there were only six months between my oldest sister Marianna's birthday and Mother and Daddy's wedding anniversary. I asked Daddy once, "Tell me how ya'll got married in August and Marianna was born in January?"

"Boy, go somewhere an' sit down. You too grown for yo' own good." That was the end of the conversation. But, I knew that they were sexually active long before they got married. They believed in replenishing the earth. And let's face it, there was not much else to do. And no money to do it. Being Black and poor still seem to go together.

I was disappointed that I would be deprived of witnessing my mother's joy regarding my biggest accomplishment. But I was more concerned about her health than anything else. The graduation was not the most important thing in the world to me. It was certainly not as important as my dear mother. I was finishing high school—not with a general diploma, but with an academic, college preparatory diploma. Imagine that: I was going to college. The first person in our house to make it to the halls of a college. My mother was so proud of me, and yet she could not be there in the flesh. She was there in spirit, though. I certainly had not done my best in high school. But I had survived and succeeded where my other siblings had failed. Their school failure was not totally their fault. They didn't seem to have the same drive. I was driven by hopes and dreams beyond my own imagination and beyond the horizons of Matoaca Road. I dreamed of becoming a doctor, an engineer, a lawyer, or somebody rich. Oh, I could dream both night and day.

We had no electricity, no running water, as I've said. There was no typewriter, and no desks to study on. So my older brother and sisters paved the way for me by trying their best to stay in school and learn. They simply could not do it. I can imagine them being teased by other students and discouraged

by some of their teachers. Disdain and condescending atti-
tudes were commonplace. They were in fact slow learners. This
was before Title I and Title V legislation. There was no special
education strategy and no Head Start program. No Individual
Educational Plans for poor Black children. This was the segregated South we were living in.

Educational and social theorists have written about it. John
Goodlad, Jean Piaget, Daniel Patrick Moynihan, and others have
theorized about achievement. The home is the most important
variable, they now say. It is what children learn at home that
determines their achievement, their success. "We can't blame
the teachers or the schools," they say. This is a copout. It is not
about blame, but advancing educational achievement. It smells
like an excuse for poor schools and ineffective teaching. If the
home is more important than the school, then almost all urban
school districts can close up shop and kiss educational excellence and achievement goodbye. The school is the one place
where some children get to eat, to read, and to play. While all
this focus has some truth to it, there seem to be other factors,
less quantifiable, that play a role in educational success: loving and smart Black teachers, dedicated parents, clean school
buildings, principals who get out of their offices and participate
in instruction by encouraging teachers, children, and parents
to partner together for the sake of the child. There are others
such as pastors, lawyers, doctors, folk who read, and then there
is luck, and a strong desire—a will to do it. This is a burdensome
gift. While the goodness and grace of God have allowed me to
be where I am today, I don't deserve anything more than my
brothers or sisters or others in the Black community. As a matter of fact, those who have graduated from high school and college and landed a good job or started a business have an even
greater burden to reach back and help somebody else along the
way. I know it sounds like a cliché. It sounds corny, even. But

it's true. My father used to have a saying that I heard often: "It's hard, but it's fair." I knew this the day I finished high school. I knew that I had been elected—chosen to be a leader. It is a terrible burden. Not even the children of Israel wanted to be elected or chosen by God because to be elected and to be rejected are one and the same. They are two sides of the same coin. Look at the story of Job: "God said to Satan, 'Have you considered my servant Job'?" (Job 1:8). This is the suffering of the innocent. Nobody remotely concerned about self-preservation wants to be on the receiving end of such a question. It's too much like being chosen. It's too close to suffering. It's like being God's Elect. Election is to suffering as *Black* skin is to *nigger*.

I had an eerie feeling on graduation day that I was losing my grip on the past and the present. I was losing my identity by forming a new one. I was changing from who I was into somebody else. I was not a new person, but a different person. I was losing my connection with those whom I loved. My sisters and brothers, my cousins. I felt like a stranger in a foreign land. A land where there were no more fields to plow, no more tobacco to prime and cure, to harvest. No more pulling weeds and watering the crops or feeding the hogs or grazing the crazy mule. There was no more following in the footsteps of my father and Uncle C. F. This was a sad and lonely day—a day of mourning in my soul. I was grieving the loss of the familiar. Familiarity sometimes breeds false comfort and satisfaction. So, my sense of place was eroding under my own feet, and the fear and sadness I felt caused me to tremble and to weep. My tears, though, were silent, just below the surface of my pain. While I wanted to cry, I could not. Neither could I smile or laugh. I had too much to think about. I was a stranger to myself and to my own people. This feeling would return every time I achieved another milestone or received another graduate degree.

My daddy was so proud the day I marched across the stage after my name was called. "Nothing will keep me from being there, son. If I can't get a ride, then I'll walk." Daddy graduated that day in June 1970. My mother graduated that same day. My siblings who had dropped out of high school also graduated that day. We all did because for the first time in our family, I had a high school diploma and it belonged to all of us. People could never look at us the same way again because James Henry, Richard's boy, Carrie Anna's son, John, Marianna, and Gloria's brother had graduated from high school. Douglas, Horace, Glenn, and Jackie's brother had earned a high school diploma.

For me, Sigmund Freud and his disciples are absolutely wrong in describing a son's relationship with his father—a son being against his father, a son's desire to replace his father. The Oedipus complex did not apply to me. There was never any subliminal hatred for my father in spite of my knowledge of his love and desire for my mother. No jealousy. In spite of the "aural repertory of lovemaking" done in the dark of night under the assumption of concealment and sleep. I loved my mother and my father more than life itself and even today when I think about them, I often begin to cry. A certain grief engulfs me, and the pain of my loss is soothed only by drifting off to sleep.

I remember when we graduated from a wood-burning stove and heater to kerosene oil. The new heater used to sit in the middle of the floor between the living room and the kitchen. By then Daddy and all of us "helpers" had added four rooms to our little two-room house. It took forever. On weeknights. Weekends. By lamplight, we worked and worked. There was still no central heat or insulation, so in winter we put old clothes, quilts, and coats on the bed to keep warm. The smell of kerosene was always in our clothes and on our skin. November through March. It was in the heat of the air. These were the smells of winter during my childhood and youth. The smells of being poor in America. The smell of Blackness in the United States.

On Sunday mornings, we often ate salt herring and mackerel patties cooked on the stove top to a crisp golden brown, pan-seared with onions and green peppers. These were the tasty delicacies that my mother would prepare. And, in summer, blackberry pies, fried corn, squash, persimmons, cucumbers, and sliced tomatoes right off the vine. Delicious. Oh, watermelons, and cantaloupes were sweet and juicy. The smells of honeysuckle and fresh tomatoes linger in my mind as I remember weltering in the grass and wallowing in the dirt, enjoying the haze of the summer's sun. Summertime. Maybe that explains why I have a love of summer. Of all the seasons, summer is by far my favorite. I learned from my father how to tell if a watermelon is ripe by the sound it makes when plucked. I could pluck a watermelon and predict its sweetness based on the sharpness or dullness of the sound. I am an expert at it, or at least I thought I was until I made a few bad predictions. Green, not ripe. Too ripe. Either one was a failure. A lapse in judgment. Then I started observing the color of the stem to determine ripeness. That was a more reliable way of doing it. If the stem is brown, then the melon is ripe. If it is a bit green, you have to wait a while. Another week or two. Good judgment is the key to a juicy, good-tasting Virginia-grown watermelon.

Summer was a time of bare feet, short pants, no shirts. Just like Huck and Jim, lying naked on the raft, floating up and down the Mississippi River. But we were only half naked, not buck naked like the two of them. I can imagine that only the shadow of the moon's glowing light could be seen in the darkness. Each passing tree or bush became a monster to the two fugitives. "We was always naked," says Huck. Huck and Jim, what a pair. So close and yet so far away from each other. That made me think of my father. *We were closer than Huck and Jim*, I thought to myself. When we had only two rooms for all of us to live in, Daddy decided to add four more rooms to our little house with his own hands. This meant that all of us had to pitch in and help. It took more than ten years to get those rooms built and before they were finished we had to sleep in them at night. Some winters were cold and airy. Everybody had to sleep with somebody. There was no such thing as sleeping by yourself. My younger siblings slept in the bed with Mama and I slept in the bed with Daddy—out in the cold unheated new part of the house. Momma and the rest of 'em slept in the room where the potbellied wood-burning heater was. Every space in the house, in the bed, and on the floor was taken. No one else could fit in the little box of a room. That's why Daddy and I slept in the part of the house that was under construction for so, so long. It's a wonder we didn't die from pneumonia or some other malady. But we survived all these physical, mental, and economic challenges. And then came our most life-changing experience. Out of the blue, my daddy got sick. Suddenly and without warning, strength turned to weakness. Daddy, the towering pillar of strength, became a frail phantom of the man I had known all my life. From that day forward, I realized that weakness is ever present even in strength. That was the day that idealism was snatched from my soul and I began to understand the meaning of my own mortality. My father's brush with death caused me to tremble with fear.

Daddy always got me to do everything that involved the public, such as going to the store to buy groceries for the family, writing letters, paying bills, going to the schools to speak to teachers. If my younger brothers Glenn and Horace got in trouble or were suspended from school, it also fell upon me to take care of things. Daddy put all his hope and trust in me from the time I was thirteen. We were poor and Daddy had to go to work because he refused to let my mother or sisters work for Mr. Driscoll, who had asked one day if Mother could wash and iron for his family. Phil Driscoll, a white man, who lived in a big plantation house across the road, came to the door one Saturday morning. I was standing in the shadows, but I could hear the conversation.

"Good morning, Richard. How you doing today?"

"We're doing OK, Mr. Phil."

"Richard, you know I was trying to get some help for my wife around the house."

"Uh, I see."

"I was wondering if I could get your wife or one of your gals to do a little cleaning and ironing a few days a week."

"Well, Phil, they got enough to do around here with all these chil'ren and all."

"I'll pay good money, one dollar for every shirt that is starched and ironed. I'll pick 'em up early and drive 'em back before nightfall," he said.

"Well, you know it ain't the money. They got enough to do here around the house and in the fields." I could see Mr. Driscoll's face turn red as Daddy turned him down flat.

"OK, Richard, if that's the way you want it. But if you change your mind, just let me know."

"All right. I'll certainly let you know." I'm sure Daddy was saying under his breath or in the hidden recesses of his mind, "Yeah, when hell freezes over. My mind will never change."

Daddy was stubborn as a mule and highly proud, too proud to ask for help or to accept any charity. We thought it was false pride, "as poor as we was." Although at the same time Mr. Driscoll would leave Christmas and Thanksgiving baskets on our front doorstep. As children, we were elated. Daddy wasn't too happy about it. But Momma was thankful for the food too.

Daddy was not about to change his mind because he had trouble working for white folks himself and he was not going to allow my mother or my sisters to work in a white man's house. He was chauvinistic and patriarchal, too, by today's standards. He felt he knew what happened to Black women in white folks' houses and no amount of money or enticements could make him think differently. So my mother never worked outside of our house. And I don't know how she could have, with all of us pulling and tugging at her twenty-four hours a day; seven days a week; three hundred sixty-five days a year. She never had a day to herself and she never complained. She didn't have time to complain. And who could she complain to? She had the "most beautifulist spirit." Sometimes she would pack us up and we would walk the quarter mile down the road to my Aunt Betty Mae's house. Aunt Betty Mae had a house full of children older than we were. All boys and one girl. And by the time I could remember her only daughter, she was married and gone. Her youngest twin boys, Timothy and Tony, were the same age as I am. My brother Doug and I were like brothers to Timothy and Tony. And my oldest brother, John Richard, was very close to two of her older boys, George and Eddie. Aunt Betty Mae was a large churchgoing woman who could cook up a storm. Her buttermilk biscuits melted in your mouth. Her fried chicken, potato salad, and cornbread were favorites of ours. She was always generous and kind to us. We were her extended family. She would say to my mother, "Carrie, you come on in here and give them chil'ren something to eat. I got plenty."

"Betty Mae, they shouldn't be hungry." Mother was being polite. She knew we were hungry and so was she. But before she could protest any longer, we had descended upon the food like vultures or a hungry brood of chickens. That was the main reason we would go to her house a few times a week, especially in spring and summertime. Mother also enjoyed talking to Aunt Betty Mae, who was a great talker. Daddy did too. She'd known Daddy and the rest of them long before coming to Virginia. They knew each other while growing up in Granville County, Creedmore, and in the Oxford, North Carolina, area. The Bass family and the Harris family went way back. Aunt Betty Mae was a Bass before she married Daddy's oldest brother, Garland. She was a counselor and a wonderful spirit to help take Mother's mind off the struggle and difficulty of being pregnant every other year. Aunt Betty Mae was older than mother, with eleven children of her own. She knew the struggle better than my mother did.

These struggles paled in comparison to the dislocation we felt when Daddy took sick. We were caught in a fog worse than the one Huck and Jim encountered when their raft capsized.

Chapter 12

Daddy's heart attack and hospitalization were very hard on all of us. I was a wreck. He was the symbol of manhood and strength. He had never been sick a day in his life. At least as far as I knew. He would tell the story of having minor surgery on his back right after his honorable discharge from the United States Army, and he always showed the small scar to us as children. A cyst or a lipoma had been excised by army doctors at the VA hospital somewhere in upstate New York. That was the story I always knew growing up. But this was different. Much more serious.

It was the summer of 1975, and I was in school trying to finish my master of divinity degree. I was in a Greek-language class for the first time. Greek language and literature. I didn't even know how to identify or pronounce the alphabet. But when Daddy got sick three or four weeks into that class, Greek became even harder. I couldn't concentrate. I could barely think straight. I couldn't focus on the memorization or the vocabulary drills. My grades plummeted. Daddy had never even been to the doctor, not to mention the hospital. And this was very serious.

It happened in the middle of the night around 2 a.m. Daddy had gotten out of bed with severe chest pains and difficulty breathing. My sister called the paramedics, who got there in about ten minutes and hauled him off to Petersburg General Hospital. These were the longest ten minutes of my young life. The doctors determined that he had suffered a heart attack, so they stabilized him and then transported him to McGuire VA

Hospital in Richmond. "Your father has suffered a severe cardiac infarction," the young emergency room physician said.

"What does that mean? Can you speak English so we can understand?"

"Yes. Mr. Harris has suffered a pretty severe heart attack. We're going to transport him to the McGuire Medical Center in Richmond where there is a team of heart specialists who can help him get better."

"Can we see him now?"

"No. I think it's best to wait until he gets settled in at McGuire. Right now, he needs to rest."

Daddy had been in the army during World War II. We were all familiar with his dog tags and the German Luger pistol he kept in the trunk with important papers, like his honorable discharge. I grew up looking at that gun and watching Daddy clean and polish it every once in a while. "Don't ever play with this gun," he would warn us.

"No, sir."

"Stay away from it. Don't touch it."

I thought about that and other things as Daddy lay there weakened by his heart attack. It was ominous and scary to me. I began to ask myself, Was Daddy going to die that very day? I have never prayed so hard in my whole life. I prayed that God would heal Daddy. And, just as God healed King Hezekiah in the Bible when he turned his face to the wall and prayed, God also healed my daddy. I still believe in miracles in spite of the Enlightenment philosophers like Immanuel Kant and G. W. F. Hegel and psychologists who suggest that man is the master of his own fate and destiny. Ralph Waldo Emerson and self-reliance be damned. I need a higher power. The drama of the self is seen in life's failures, which are many.

I was in a seminary now. Graduate professional school. Daddy was mighty proud. While I had learned to cuss in high school, in the seminary I learned that the sacred and the profane were not opposites, but twin elements that engulf the same mind and body. Two sides of the self where each side was hiding from the other. We are all dialectical beings. Praying one moment and cussing the next.

"Boy, I have forgotten more than you know," Daddy would say as a retort to my correcting his grammar or some word he had used incorrectly. His sisters, my aunts, used to hate it when I would tell Daddy, "You mean they *were*, not they *was*." Daddy would smile. Unfazed by my newfound knowledge and prevailing ignorance, he would rub me on the head as a sign of encouragement.

"Richard, you need to slap that boy for correcting you like that."

"Oh, it's OK, Joyce. He don't know no better and besides I don't mind it."

"No. It's not right and you need to teach him to respect his elders."

"He just learned that in school, so he's trying to show me what he learned."

"He needs a whipping. That's what he needs," my aunt would say.

Daddy always knew that I loved him more than my words could express. And I had nothing but respect, absolute respect for my daddy. To me, he was taller than the Blue Ridge Mountains and higher than the clouds in the sky. Daddy had no earthly equal.

I thought about all of that when I saw Daddy hooked up to the monitors in the intensive care unit. There were machines monitoring his heart, oxygen, pulse rate, and blood pressure. There were IVs in his arms and tubes in his nose to give him oxygen. Daddy was sick and I was scared. Worse than that, there was nothing I could do. I wanted to take his place. Let me be sick, but not Daddy. I was crying and bleeding inside. It was a crisis for our family. The strong man who was able to do all things according to my imagination was lying prostrate in a hospital room. Helpless. Frail. Weak. Human, all too human, on the brink of death. The family's patriarch was no longer able to stand on his own. The strong man was no longer strong. He needed help to do something as simple as breathe. I began to think about the thousand times our mother would say to me and my brothers and sisters whenever we misbehaved, "I'm gonna tell your daddy on you when he comes home." That was enough to make us all stand in fear. Momma's saying those threatening words was enough for us to straighten up and act right for a whole day.

The male presence alone is not enough to help constitute a healthy family, though. A man in the house who is not loving, but abusive, violent, and domineering is more harmful than helpful. Those who argue for male presence without regard to the quality of that presence propagate a patriarchy that scapegoats the single mother. I have learned that patriarchy as a word, a concept, and a practice is laden with complexities. The screen for talking about this subject includes identity, oppression, privilege, power, race, sex, class, caste, love, family, etc. We have a tendency to be confounded in our understanding of patriarchy because we underestimate the complexities and limit our interpretation to race, gender, or class without recognizing the correlation or interface between patriarchy and the making and unmaking of our identity. Patriarchy is so pervasive that it often takes on elusive forms that are not only difficult to grasp but also difficult to identify. For example, society and the family often describe certain male behaviors and practices as masculine and inoffensive, while others are seen as effeminate and undesirable. Actions such as crying or reading are feminine while stoic disinterest and cussing are said to be masculine. Even skin color is an indicator of a patriarchal system that values lighter-complexioned Blacks because their skin tone and hair texture are closer to whites. This fact itself shows how white supremacy is the matrix out of which patriarchy emerges and mutates throughout the family, church, school, and culture.

When I was growing up in the 1960s, children who had light skin were favored by teachers, and all of us boys migrated toward lighter-skinned girls because the school culture projected the thesis that lighter skin translated into beauty, academic achievement, and superior school performance. The partial divestiture of this mentality was accomplished through slogans in the late sixties like "Black Is Beautiful" or James Brown's song, "Say It Loud, I'm Black and I'm Proud." Our pastor's wife, who grew up in North Carolina in the forties and fifties, tells of how she was refused the honor of valedictorian in her school because of her dark complexion, even though she had the highest grade point average. These actions were perpetrated by Black educators against other Blacks who were not as aesthetically appealing according to the prevailing popular culture mindset; bell hooks calls this the "patriarchal color caste" within the Black family and community. I have heard similar stories about churches in Virginia that were color-struck, only securing pastors who were light-skinned males. This psychology is also seen among Black males who are only interested in dating and marrying women who are light-complexioned with a certain hair texture—although many Blacks today use texturizer and extensions in their hair. It's hard to know what is authentic and what is not.

When I was in seminary in the mid-seventies, all of the professors were male and ninety-nine percent of the student body was also male. Even today, a significant majority of professional schools are headed by males and those who occupy the highest academic rank are also male. As I mentioned earlier, when I was in elementary school, all of the teachers were female and the only males in the school were the principal and the custodian. When I was thirteen years old, my parents put certain responsibilities for the entire family on my shoulders. Was this an abdication of responsibility on their part, and an increasing load on me? I guarantee that it was an increasing load on me. But I'm not so sure it was abdication of responsibility on their part. Growing up in rural central Virginia as farmers and laborers, my daddy and his brothers had migrated from Vance County, North Carolina, to Virginia in the early 1940s. My father was a strong man and, in my view, very responsible and compassionate, but not any more responsible and compassionate than my mother. He was extremely nervous and easily excited when it came to us. It was clear that my mother adored him and acceded certain things to our father, who was indeed the dominant force in our household. This was a positive attribute and does not qualify as patriarchy in any negative sense, but in a very positive way; it was an example of male responsibility as protector of the family, a provider and a moral example who expressed love toward our mother and all of us—most of the time.

So, in this positive affirming sense, my father was patriarchal, possessing the critical trait of parental love. Our father's love accommodated the strong arm of protection and authority that his persona embodied as well as that bestowed on him by our mother, who would often intone, "When your daddy comes home, I'm going to tell him how bad you been today." I have struggled with describing our father as patriarchal because the term is often negative in literature, but my memories of my father as positive, loving, and kind complicate my understanding of the concept and practice of patriarchy. I cannot help but question, however, the fact that my mother bore eleven children out of compliance to a system of patriarchy in a society that influences the family structure as well as sexual behavior and the submission of women to the will of the male or father. This submission is often out of love, though sometimes out of fear—both love and fear being strong emotional determinates of behavior. In many ways love and fear mimic each other and it is up to us to know and recognize the difference. I loved my father; I also feared him. Life is never so easy as to be full of love all the time. Love is a fleeting emotion, and in many ways, it is always in competition with fear. To understand the difference between the two is the nature of wisdom. "The fear of the Lord is the beginning of wisdom, and knowledge of the Holy One is understanding" (Prov 9:10).

Chapter 13

On August 15, 1988, a placid, warm, and sultry summer day, my wife, children, and I decided to drive from Norfolk to Atlanta. It was hot. We had a new Datsun B210 hatchback, which was comfortable enough for the four of us. Our two boys were six and two years old. Any trip over one hundred miles was a journey. It was an adventure like traveling up the Mississippi. We stopped overnight in the Queen City, Charlotte, North Carolina, and then by mid-morning the next day we headed to Atlanta. Interstate 85 South was crowded, but the drive was pastoral and peaceful. The children always fell asleep as soon as the wheels hit the road. They could sleep for hours. Riding was like a sedative.

We got to Atlanta by early evening and settled into our hotel room. We toured the city—CNN headquarters, the Coca-Cola plant—and spent the next full day at the mall. It was perfect pleasure and leisure. I was worry-free. We spent the next day at the Martin Luther King Jr. Center and at Morehouse College where King had gone to school. Atlanta was bustling and thriving.

"Atlanta is beginning to look a bit like New York," I said to my wife.

"Not exactly. It doesn't feel like New York to me. It's not as fast," she said.

As a country boy, I had only been to Atlanta one other time. It was two years earlier. The lights, the skyscrapers, Peachtree Street, the Braves Stadium. The Atlanta Falcons. Ted Turner.

TNT. All made me happy. Little did I know what sorrows that day had in store for me.

As soon as we arrived back home, in Norfolk, Virginia, I sensed something was wrong because my mother-in-law was at our house waiting for us. This was unusual. Very unusual. She had a key, but to my knowledge, she never used it. When she opened the door, I saw that her face was etched with sympathy.

"I have something to tell you. Bad news."

"Yes ma'am, what is it?"

"Your sister Vanessa called. She said that your daddy died this morning. He was at her house when he collapsed and fell to the floor."

"Oh, no! No-o-o."

"The paramedics came, but there was nothing they could do."

I was devastated by the words, "Your daddy died this morning." I felt as if I had been thrown into the abyss; I had been hurled into the swirling winds of chaos. I slumped down into a chair, surrounded by my wife and her mother, and yet I felt utterly alone. An aloneness brought on by the death of my father. Not only that, time stopped me in my tracks as I thought, *There is no escape from death. It is more than a possibility. It is fact of life.*

It is a certainty for all human beings. Heidegger's *Sein und Zeit* and his concept of Dasein were gradually becoming clear to me. What I didn't understand in ten years of graduate study in theology and philosophy had come to light in a few piercing words: "Your daddy died today."

I wish I could say that grief has let go of me, but I can't. I'm still not prepared, and I feel that I'll never be prepared for this. It has been more than thirty years now since that hot August day in 1988—but at times, it feels like yesterday. Recently, I was giving a lecture at Virginia Union University, and at the end of the presentation, someone in the audience asked me a question.

In response to the question, I invoked my father's name and his standard admonition to everybody in the house to "sit down and be quiet while James Henry works on his sermon." Tears began to well up in my eyes as I became choked up with emotion. Just that brief memory from deep inside my soul pushed forth an unspeakable sorrow. At that moment, I could not fathom the absurd indifference of Albert Camus's main character Mersault's opening statement in his novel *The Stranger*: "Maman died today. Or yesterday maybe, I don't know."

I was the absolute opposite. I shall always know the day my daddy died. And the day my momma died. That I do know for certain. Daddy died on August 18, 1988, and Mother died on April 5, 1989, just eight months apart. Both too soon and too close together!

My mother was a quiet person possessed by a very humble spirit. She made do with little or nothing in terms of clothes and shoes and other material things. She didn't wear shoes in the summertime and neither did we. She loved to go to church and enjoyed the fellowship of her family and friends. She was not as close to her sisters as she was to her youngest brother David, who would stop by our house once or twice a week. Uncle David and my great uncle Willie took special interest in visiting Mother and Daddy. They would sit around the potbelly stove and talk for hours. Maxwell House coffee was the favorite drink for the adults, as Kool-Aid was for the children.

"Carrie Anna, how you doing today? It's good to see you."

"I'm doing OK, brother," she would say.

"You need anything for all these chil'ren?"

"No, they doing all right. Just keep me real busy."

"I can see that, Carrie Anna," he would say as he sipped his coffee.

Mother's quiet spirit could only be wrangled by my brother's tattling tongue. John Richard had a disease of telling things that were meant to be refrigerated or dead on arrival. My maternal grandma, Susie Jones, was lured into an altercation with her neighbor Ms. Goldie T. because of the mushy mouth of my brother. His untamed tongue could set ablaze the most placid and peaceful places.

"Big Mama, I heard Ms. Goldie T. say something bad about you and Big Papa," John whispered to our grandmother.

"What did she say, Johnnie?"

"She called you a name—a bad name."

"I'll see what she has to say to my face," Big Mama said as she grabbed Big Papa's hat and coat and marched up the road to Ms. Goldie T.'s house. It was too far away for me to see what happened once she got there, but John Richard was always at the center of confusion because he talked too much with too little information. But, in the spirit of Twain, "that ain't the worst."

One day after Daddy and John Richard came home from a long day of working in the woods, cutting and hauling pulpwood, my brother told my mother about something that took place while they were at work.

"Momma, Daddy and 'em were talking about your momma and Uncle David in the woods today," John Richard said.

"What do you mean, John Richard?"

"Daddy and 'em were saying that the Joneses, the Lewises, and the Browns all came from the same household. They were kissing cousins."

"He don't know nothing about my family," said mother. "Richard, what was that ya'll was talking about in the woods today?"

"Carrie, that boy don't know what he's talking about. Nobody was talking 'bout your peoples," Daddy assured her.

But that was not good enough. Mother was standing in Daddy's face, acting bolder than I had ever seen her. And Daddy was the epitome of humility as he walked out the door to get some fresh air. I interpreted his behavior as a sign of guilt. My brother had put Daddy in an awkward situation and caused my mother to get uncharacteristically angry. She kept arguing as Daddy stepped onto the grass in the front yard.

"Devil take your Black skin, Richard Harris," Mother said as she retreated into the house. With these words, Mother had cursed Daddy in her own way. She didn't pursue it because she didn't fully believe my brother John Richard, either. She knew that he was prone to gossip and exaggeration. Because of that she warned my brother with these words: "A dog that brings a bone will also carry a bone."

That day I saw a rare side of both of my parents because they seldom argued. I saw Mother stand up to Daddy, and I saw Daddy cower to a truth that he could not escape.

While I was close to my mother, I was in fact a "daddy's boy." As a child, I used to pray that nothing would ever happen to my daddy. I would stick to him like white on rice or like tar on an ol' tin roof. Even when Daddy went to the bathroom, I would go with him and stand beside him until he finished doing what he was there to do. I loved my daddy. He was like a god.

Soon after Daddy's funeral, my mother became very sick. She probably had been sick for a while but kept it to herself. My sisters and brothers took her to doctor after doctor where it was finally determined that she had late-stage colon cancer. She was sixty-four years old so Medicare was able to help after several months. She had one surgery at Petersburg General and was later transferred to the Massey Cancer Center at the Medical College of Virginia. While in the Richmond hospital this last time, and before I could get to visit her again, she died in the middle of the night, alone. No relatives. Not that they could have helped. But this was one time that I disagreed with Sigmund Freud "that the relatives can be worse than the disease." My sister Vanessa called me after midnight that night. I felt a sense of dread as soon as the phone rang. It was April 5, 1989—less than a year after we had buried Daddy.

"James Henry, the chaplain from the MCV hospital just called. Momma died a short time ago." She was crying, softly. I could sense her anguish and pain. My sister is the epitome of calmness and strength, but this was hard on her. My parents had lived with her for nearly a year while their house was being repaired.

"Ah, do you know what happened?"

"No. I went to visit her today after I got out of school. She seemed OK. They were planning to start her chemotherapy treatments tomorrow."

"I'm so shocked. I know Mother was sick. Very sick. But, I just didn't . . . I didn't think she was at death's door. I would have been there, you know. I could have . . ."

"I know, brother. I wish I had been there too. When I told her I'd see her tomorrow, Momma just smiled and squeezed my hand. That's the way she was, you know. Always quiet. Never making a fuss."

"I know. I should have been there. I could have been there . . . if . . ."

The tears began to flow. I was weakened by my own words. My own guilt. My own fear. In less than nine months, both my father and mother had passed away. Daddy in August 1988 and Mother in April 1989, just days after her sixty-fifth birthday. Daddy was sixty-eight when he died. The words of the psalmist came back to me: "Lord, you have been our dwelling place in all generations. . . . The days of our life are seventy years, or perhaps eighty, if we are strong: Even then their span is only toil and trouble: They are soon gone, and we fly away."

I thought about all the laughter and the cries. All the joys and the sorrows. I thought about the fact that neither Daddy nor Mother, without a raffish or reprobate bone in their bodies, lived to see the age of seventy. This was a tragedy to me. Two sweet, kind-hearted people who struggled all of their lives to make ends meet, to gain the respect of others, to provide us with a sense of pride—dead. Never to speak again. Never to ask me what I thought about this or that idea or person. As time has elapsed, I must confess that I do hear them speaking to me in my imagination. They are not dead because life and death are one. I think. Maybe, maybe not. In the silence of my spirit or on a day when I'm riding past a farm where the fields are full of corn or tobacco and the sky is about to burst with rain, I can see them in the shape of a cloud. And, on days when I'm visiting the sick members of the church or walking past the maternity ward, I can hear them in the cry of a newborn baby or when I'm sitting on the porch or on the deck, I hear their voices in the melodic sounds of the birds calling my name, *James Henry . . . James Henry . . .* And then I know that God's spirit infuses the earth with the oneness of both life and death. When I walk every morning in the freshness of daybreak, on occasion I talk with them about my life as we walk together.

Chapter 14

One day as the semester was coming to a close, and we had discussed Huck's struggle between a good heart versus a deformed conscience, and his belief that preachers and swindlers were one and the same, I asked the professor and the class about the peculiar relationship between Huck and Jim. In the language of Shelley Fisher Fishkin, the question had been posed: Was Huck Black? And I ventured to ask, Was Huck gay? Had anyone ever thought about this? It seemed like a reasonable area of inquiry, devoid of any moral judgment. What was to be made of the fact that Jim often called Huck "honey"? I asked. I continued, "And many days and nights Huck and Jim lay naked on the raft smoking and talking about all kinds of things as they drifted up and down the Mississippi."

There was silence in the room, so I went on pressing my case to the point of annoyance. Like a gadfly or a philosopher like Socrates or Plato. I pointed out that Huck did some crossdressing with Jim's help. And he practiced how to walk and talk like a girl—although he was not too good at it. And even Jim, with the help of the Duke, had been dressed up in a "long curtain-calico gown." I was being antagonistic for the sake of enlightenment. I also recognized that there was a lot in the text that had more than one clear meaning and Huck and Jim's love language could be grounded in *eros*. Intellectual curiosity is in my nature and the surplus of meaning seems natural to me. I thought I was being Socratic or even Hegelian. Maieutic. This was indeed the most callous thing that could be said about such an iconic protagonist. I was doing a Huck. No! I was "out-hucking" Huck. I was also emulating Mark Twain by being the consummate contrarian. It was a blasphemous, unorthodox inquiry. Twain to the core. It was a "Twaining" of Mark Twain.

The truth is there was more to it than simple mischief, though. It was irony *par excellence.* I was reflecting upon Greek philosophy, especially *The Symposium* by Plato, where homo-erotic discussions of *eros* permeate the speeches of Phaedrus, Eryximachus, Aristophanes, Agathon, and Socrates. Plato was right: everyone turns into a poet when touched by *eros*, whether it is Athenian male-male affection of the loved and the lover or the desire for the other mythic half of the self. So it could be argued that Huck and Jim's relationship is, in a Greek sense, a type of homoeroticism where sexual and erotic desires are directed at the other without regard to gender. In Greek culture and during that time, the adult male lover of a pubescent boy could be married to a woman. I put two and two together. Jim was married with children. Huck was a budding adolescent. The problem with this Athenian reflection is that Jim was an adult slave and his slave status obviated his adulthood and his manhood. He was the de jure boy. Huck was the man. The boy is the object of the man's desire. Could Jim be Huck's other half? This was my imagination gone wild. Or was it? Surely, it didn't originate with me. Leslie Fiedler in his essay "Come Back to the Raft Ag'in, Huck Honey," shows that he is the expert on archetypal love between the white male and the Black male; the myth of the nigger and the white boy as a symbol of unity. This has always been controversial, but Fiedler was bold enough to write it down, long before I brought it up in class that day.

My question about Huck's and Jim's sexuality was not grounded in the notion of homosexuality advanced by psycho-analysts Sigmund Freud or Carl Jung. Gender identity was not the issue. No, I was thinking outside the box. I reasoned that I could take this a few steps further. And so I did. Why not bring some other insightful voices into the provocative conversation?

I thought of the poem "Diving into the Wreck" by Adrienne Rich and its symbols of sexuality, myth, and self-exploration as a perfect analogy to Huck and Jim's relationship.* It spawned other thoughts about the sources of the self, the psychology and sociology of the self, and how my own life felt wrecked. The first few stanzas of Rich's poem suggest to me that the subject is experiencing a process of individuation and self-understanding. The language in the poem's "book of myths" suggests that the author knows something about the symbolic projections of folk like Jim's and Huck's hopes, values, fears, and aspirations. Rich's knowledge regarding the inherent assumptions of myths about women enables her to proceed to examine her own life with the same power and determination with which Jacques Cousteau examined the deep, dark, dangerous depths of the sea. Also, there are other images of the phallic symbol in the language of the third stanza—that is, "edge of the knife-blade."

First having read the book of myths,
and loaded the camera,
and checked the edge of the knife-blade,
I put on
the body-armor of black rubber
the absurd flippers
the grave and awkward mask.

Maybe I was on a tangent, but I kept on reaching, extending my critical blasphemous literary lens. I was really enjoying this analysis—this excursus. When one is clothed, nakedness is symbolized by the face. Uncovered. Unprotected. The face, unlike

---

* The section about "Diving Into the Wreck" by Rich is similar to what I wrote in *No Longer Bound*. Eugene, Oregon: Cascade Books. 2013.

the rest of the body, is obvious and open to public examination. But Huck and Jim took their clothes off much like the Greeks in their bath houses during the reign of Demetrius I. So, nakedness is ultimately symbolized by the penis. The phallus. The knife-blade. A new image of the self. I was on a roll. My mind raced to the edge of interpretation as I kept comparing Huck and Jim's behavior to what was going on in the powerful poem "Diving into the Wreck." Maybe there was no relationship, but I forced the possibility, through my reasoned imagination, and I began to mourn the death of the image of Huck and Jim's innocence. I could feel the tension in the class. There was a thick, cold silence that was more piercing than any vehement verbal objection.

I thought of Freudian psychoanalysis. Sexual images leap forth from almost every line of Rich's poem, especially in the words

checked the edge of the knife-blade,
I put on
the body-armor of black rubber

This is symbolism for the preparation to commence a sexual act. Or, so I imagined. Just like floating on the raft "buck naked." No. This is just creativity gone awry. Fictive thinking. Creative imagination. And, yet I knew that for Sigmund Freud, almost every act or object has a sexual meaning or interpretation; however, the language of this poem suggests that whatever the subject is doing is private and individual, and somewhat forced or against the will of the subject. This is an internal struggle with the self—a battle between the id and the superego being mediated by the rational, governing power of the ego. I believe the following lines attest to this introspective interpretation: "I am having to do this not like Cousteau with his assiduous team aboard the sun-flooded schooner but here alone."

The contrast with Cousteau said to me that this is not a literal voyage but a symbolic search for the authentic self, and no amount of armor is sufficient to protect one from the collateral damage of the wreck. Huck and Jim's voyage up and down the Mississippi River is an exercise in mythmaking. Nobody will disagree with that interpretation. A landless journey to freedom. A freedom that doesn't exist anywhere else except on the raft. Not in Missouri. Not in Ohio. Not in any state, slave or free. Only on the river, where the laws of nature govern the events, can Huck and Jim ever be truly free on American soil. I'm sorry, I mean American waters.

Unlike Cousteau with a team of industrious, hard-working divers on an open-deck sailing vessel, the subject in "Wreck" is here alone in the dark depths of Rich's own troubled self, a place where there is no sunlight and maybe no hope. And yet, "there is a ladder," a symbol of rescue—a means to escape. Like the Mississippi River. This is a ladder—that is, "always there hanging innocently." And "we know what it is for, we who have used it." This ladder is indeed a means by which one can pierce the deep consciousness of the mind and body. This is not the first time that the subject has embarked on this journey toward knowledge of the inner self, and knowledge of others. Even carnal knowledge. The knowledge of good and evil. Body and soul. Freedom.

The language in the line "I go down rung after rung and still the oxygen immerses me" has a postmodern tone of oral sexuality to it, maybe the influence of Freud upon us all. Also, the words "As there is no one to tell me when the ocean will begin" reflect a child-like spirit, a desire to be told by some authoritative voice the meaning of life. This poem, like the journey of Huck and Jim, seems to me to be about the quest for identity—even sexual identity. This is not only Freudian and Jungian, inasmuch as the issues of sexuality and consciousness permeate the symbolic language, but it is also Greek. I thought of Zeus. This is certainly a union of the two entities, as the "circle" suggests. The final stanzas reflect a collectivity, a unity within the individuated self: "We are, I am, you are . . . the one who find our way . . ."

Notice the language: not "my way" but "our way."

In the way that *Adventures of Huckleberry Finn* creates or replicates a certain type of boyhood story, Rich's poem is filled with archetypal images of water as seen in the ocean and the sea. Adventure. For Carl Jung, the master of archetypes, water is the chief symbol of the unconscious as well as the harbinger of images of creation, purification, birth-death-resurrection, and fertility:

The sea is another story, the sea is not a questioning power.

The sea and the Mississippi River are one.

"Diving into the Wreck" is filled with images of water. We often think of divers as deep-sea divers, explorers of the oceans, seas, and rivers. Much like Huck and Jim, who are indeed in a wreck, at times, literally so. The very act of diving conjures images of water. The Mississippi River. The sea is a symbol of mystery and the unconscious. The sun, on the other hand, is a symbol of consciousness, creative energy, and spiritual vision. Adrienne Rich uses the image of the sun: "aboard the sun-flooded schooner" and "the drowned face always staring toward the sun."

Huck and Jim often lie naked on the raft soaking up the sun's energy and the moon's magic during the dark quiet of night. The connections are right there for us to see. Don't you think? Use your imagination.

Rich's poem is about the quest for wholeness while being surrounded by both death and life. Idealism has been shattered

by the reality principle. Isn't that what has happened to Huck
and Jim? The archetypal image of the circle suggests the nature
of this struggle toward unity:

We circle silently
about the wreck
we dive into the hold.
I am she: I am he

The yang-yin image seems to be achieved in the preceding lines. The union of the opposite forces of the masculine (yang) and the feminine (yin), conscious mind and the
unconscious, activity and passivity, have been achieved. What
a complex and powerful poem! Almost as complex as Twain
himself and almost as complex as the relationship between
Huck and Jim. Between slave and master. Between freedom
and oppression. Between the self and sexuality.

Well, I said what I said and wrote my thoughts down on
paper because these were the things that informed my desire
to speak and write. To explore the meaning of Huck and Jim's
nakedness and their strange bond. I wanted to explore the dialectic between their freedom and their bondage. Their relationship was a metaphor just like the river. Two males naked on a
raft floating free as birds up and down the Mississippi River.
There would be nothing really disturbing about that except that
Huck is white and Jim is called a nigger. A slave in search of
freedom and a white boy in search of a different kind of freedom. What's wrong with that except they are on the river going
South. The raft is a homegoing in the wrong direction:

We said there warn't no home like the raft, after all. Other places
do seem so cramped up and smothery, but a raft don't. You feel
mighty free and easy and comfortable on a raft.

The memory of my classmates' contorted faces still haunts me. The class was flabbergasted. Mouths fell open and jaws sank low. Silent shock and disgust pervaded every line in their faces. Silence engulfed the room. The stares of disbelief spoke from their eyes and an array of deeply ingrained furrows was plastered across their brows. I was no doubt brazen and callous, and bold to pose such an awful question. I was totally politically incorrect. This was a taunting and terrifying line of reasoning. Sacrilege was my crime. I was indeed a literary heretic. I was

> the awfulest and old gray-headed nabob in the state. . . . I was a p'fessor in a college, and could talk all kinds of languages.

The question of Jim's and Huck's sexuality is nuanced throughout the novel *Adventures of Huckleberry Finn*. But this was one adventure that I saw I had taken too far as soon as I said it; I even dared to write it in my formal essay. I was being mischievous to some extent, much like Twain and Huck. I also recognized that it was probably a forbidden subject. And, was I ever right. But I reasoned that if Mark Twain could be ironic and satirical, then I certainly could inject a bit of sardonic humor into the discussion. My own irony at that. Maybe it was fact, not fiction. Maybe not. But, again, I ran up against a solid brick wall; it was a fortress of protection. These folk were protecting the public interest. The tradition. They had read the propaganda era elevation of *Huckleberry Finn* by the pantheon of admirers: Lionel Trilling, T. S. Eliot, and Joseph Wood Krutch. Maintaining the myth, like the devotees of Edgar Allan Poe or Thomas Jefferson or American democracy, was their American duty: *We hold these truths to be self-evident.* Don't we?

Mine was blasphemy. How in the sacred name of God or Yahweh could I even fix my mouth to utter such an unholy and uncouthly phrased question about the most canonized of American literary characters—Huckleberry Finn, and his creator and co-conspirator Mark Twain. Wasn't I supposed to know that Huck is the epitome of boyhood masculinity? Yes, we all are supposed to know that. I felt that for my fellow classmates it didn't really matter about Jim. He was just another nigger who could be sacrificed at the altar of literary criticism. Sure, he could be gay or something else. It did not matter. He was a runaway slave. The Black body during slavery was the white man's fetish. The white woman's fetish too. The physical body and its anatomy were their fantasy and their possession. Chattel property. So, Jim could easily be a sex object or he could be asexual or bisexual or homosexual and it would cause no real stir. A male prostitute, even. But, Huck—oh, no! That would be un-American. Untrue. Unbelievable. Unlearned. Unacceptable. Unchristian. Unenlightened. The reaction to my question proved that Huck's authentic masculine boyhood must always be protected and maintained for the sake of posterity. For God's sake and for the sake of humanity. This is classic American literature. And yet, I had read Plato's masterpiece on Eros, *The Symposium*, while everyone else pretended that Greek and Athenian literature had no application to *Adventures of Huckleberry Finn*.

"It was just a thought," I said. But I had committed a sin on the order of violating one of the Ten Commandments—adultery or even murder.

Either way, it was horrendous and almost unforgivable. I had brought up a subject that was only whispered about by the bourgeoisie—never verbalized in adult, cultured settings. It proved to be forbidden, even in the halls of academia. I thought of what Huck would say: "Well, dad blame it. Blow me down."

Chapter 15

Today is another day of the Mark Twain seminar. One more class meeting and the semester will be over. We are in the final stretch of a long, hard semester where race, identity, sexuality, religion, smoking, lying, freedom, moral consciousness, comedy, and incipient tragedy have been discussed at one time or another. I have to get up early to get my mental bearings. It's a challenge to get ready for what lies ahead. So, I get up at 7:00 a.m. "gapping and stretching," to get my mind ready for a class that doesn't start until 4:00 p.m. I get strength and energy from the beauty and freshness of the morning. There is something mystical and beautiful about the early morning. It is untethered by the fetid scents of a day grown old. The morning is a new birth. The wind, like the breath of God, blowing upon the face of the earth. The sweet smell of the air breezing through the trees makes me intoxicated with the love for life. The dew drops on the grass, responding to the light of the sun as it "sifted down through the leaves." Oh, the leaves of October and November arrayed in orange, brown, yellow, red, and rust freckled to the ground. The colors of nature reflect the wonder of God. I take a deep breath to absorb the sounds of solitude and inhale the taste of the autumn air. It brings back memories of my childhood. It creates a sensation in my nostrils and in my consciousness. I can suddenly smell and taste the fragrances of bread cooked on the stove top. I can smell the white pinto beans and the turnip greens we ate almost every day. We were vegetarians by necessity, not by desire.

I love the morning air, the breeze in the trees, and the sweetness of daybreak bursting forth from the sun. After walking my ritualistic two miles to get the blood circulating, I have a clarity of mind and thought that comes from a deep love and respect for the morning light. The morning sun, the morning rain, and the morning air have been good to me. I need to feel the arms of nature massaging my body and my soul. This is a type of pantheism that overwhelms me and balances my weakness with a strength that has nothing to do with my frail mind and body.

Then, almost before I knew it, the time for class arrived. After walking about ten city blocks to get to class, I was ready to engage in the subject for the day—the continued discussion of *Adventures of Huckleberry Finn*. Comparative analysis. I've done all the readings, the critical reviews, the mountain of research on the subject. In class, the professor asks me, "James, how are you doing with your research?"

"I'm right on schedule. My thesis is clear and concise," I said.

"OK, tell us about it. What exactly is your thesis?" I begin to speak in what my daddy would call "highfalutin' language." It was pretty unconventional. Heavy stuff. Before proceeding, I let the class know that I have been impressed by so much in the book, especially the very moving story of the accident in the fog when Jim and Huck are separated and Huck plays a mean trick on Jim. Jim's final speech is riveting—filled with wisdom and deep emotion that springs to the surface:

> He looked at me steady without ever smiling and says:
>
> "What do dey stan' for? I's gwyne to tell you. When I got all wore out, wid work, en wid de callin' for you, en went to sleep, my heart wuz mos' broke bekase you wuz los', en I didn' k'yer no mo' what become er me en de raf'. En when I wake' up en fine you back agin, all safe en soun'; de tears come en I could a got down on my knees en kiss' yo' foot I's so thankful. En all you wuz thinking

'bout, wuz how you could make a fool of ole Jim wid a lie. Dat truck dah is *trash*; en trash is what people is dat puts dirt on de head er dey fren's en makes 'em ashamed."

Then he got up, slow, and walked to the wigwarm, and went in there, without saying anything but that. But that was enough. It made me feel so mean I could almost kissed his foot to get him to take it back.

It was fifteen minutes before I could work myself up to go and humble myself to a nigger—but I done it, and I warn't ever sorry for it afterwards, neither. I didn't do him no more mean tricks, and I wouldn't done that one if I'd a knowed it would make him feel that way.

Not even Jim's eloquent, thoughtful, and compelling speech could change Huck's language in Twain's mind: "humble myself to a nigger."

After that digression, I proceeded to talk about my controversial thesis.

"The ubiquitous use of *nigger* by Twain is the basic reason why his novel has attained the status of an American classic. *Nigger* is an American invention and its use by whites describes the nature and meaning of American democracy, constitutionality, and culture. In short, white Americans' use of the word *nigger* is tantamount to describing what makes America, America. Mark Twain knew this, and he too capitalized on it. This made him complicit in propagating America's white supremacist and capitalist culture." The class gasped for air. Folk were squirming. I could see and feel the tension. Alert: oxygen masks needed. Without ever using the term, I had introduced the all-white class to critical race theory by claiming that Mark Twain, the book *Adventures of Huckleberry Finn*, and the society and culture that constructed the word *nigger* are all grounded in racism.

Andrew, a classmate who really looks a lot like Mark Twain to me because of his bushy hair, said, "Well, that is a very intriguing perspective. It's going to be hard to prove, but I like the thesis."

Melissa, a bubbly and freckled-face white girl in her early twenties, chimed, "James, that's great. I think I can see your point, but . . ."

"Thank you, Melissa. You too, Andrew. I know this is provocative and controversial, but let's try to expand our horizons here."

"The problem is that few people think of Twain as a racist: not Toni Morrison, not James Baldwin, not Edward P. Jones, hardly anybody," offered another classmate, a high school English teacher in Henrico County Public Schools.

"I know. And I'm reluctant to make this claim because Twain was such a generous character toward Blacks. And he criticized whites just as well."

"Yes," said the professor. "You know he sponsored the first Black student to attend Yale Law School." I hadn't known that little historical fact, but I pretended I did.

"Yes, I'm aware of his benevolent acts of kindness towards particular individuals and his genuine interest in exposing the hypocrisy of the Gilded Age," I said.

"Well, your claim is a bold and dangerous one," said the lawyer in the class.

"I know it is. But Twain himself was a bold and dangerous fella. He was also very much interested in success and wealth, and I claim that his use of *nigger* outweighed his diatribes against religion, high society, hypocrisy, and the establishment. How many times do you have to use the word *nigger* to make your point? You answer me on that," I said rhetorically.

"Say a bit more, James," said another student. "Because I think you are on the wrong track here."

"I could be. But, I may not be. Only time will tell."

"James, this is going to take a lot of explanation," said another student.

"What I mean is that Twain's use of *nigger*, so thoroughly embedded in his text, obviates his other critiques of the mind of the South and the North. All over the world for that matter. Even irony or satire does not soften the use of the word. The word is still *n-i-g-g-e-r*. It's on almost every page of the book! That made Twain something of a genius and open to being called a racist."

Another student said, "James, that is brilliant! I've never heard anyone make such a case. Go for it!" And so I went for it. I lit out upon the uncharted, dangerous territory.

It is a part of white culture to embed racism in their religion. The white church has historically been in complicity with white supremacy, especially as it related to Blacks during slavery. The white church provided the justification for making slaves less than human by theorizing that slavery was ordained by God. This is one of the concerns Mark Twain expresses in *Adventures of Huckleberry Finn*. The feud between the Shepherdsons and the Grangerfords is indicative of Twain's view that white folks' religion was a sham created to accommodate their cultural biases, prejudices, and hatred toward one another and the Other. In *Adventures of Huckleberry Finn* going to church was a civic duty totally disconnected from any moral, ethical, or Christian responsibility. Twain describes a church scene:

> Next Sunday we all went to church, about three mile, every-body a horseback. The men took their guns along, so did Buck, and kept them between their knees or stood them handy against the wall. The Shepherdsons done the same. It was pretty ornery preaching—all about brotherly love and such-like tiresomeness, but everybody said it was a good sermon, and they all talked it over, going home, and had such a powerful lot to say about faith, and good works, and free grace, and preforeordestination, and I

don't know what all, that it did seem to me to be one of the roughest Sundays I had run across yet.

While all of these folk went to church and tolerated the sermon that was designed to reinforce the cultural mores and practices of the people, there was no discussion of the real issues like slavery, human dignity, or correlating "free grace" with the freedom of slaves. Twain thought it was laughable. A big joke. A hoax. Going to church and the use of *nigger* are as American as apple pie. In the same chapter, Huck, in describing the false aristocracy of the Grangerfords, says,

> Each person had their own nigger to wait on them—Buck, too. My nigger had a monstrous easy time, because I warn't used to having anybody do anything for me, but Buck's was on the jump most of the time.

Twain demonstrates how the word *nigger* was ingrained in the language of white American culture. How the presumption of white supremacy is clearly related to the use of the word *nigger*. So I reasoned.

The relationship between slavery and skin color permeates the history of Blacks in America. That's a given. As a matter of fact, Black folks' religion and culture are directly related to this Du Boisian "double consciousness" and to race, which has always been, and still is, a dominant issue in American life. One's Blackness forever impacts any lived understanding of culture, philosophy, ethics, and social reality. Du Bois's most famous statement is this:

> From the double life every American Negro must live. . . . The worlds within and without. . . . Such a double life with double thoughts, double duties, and double social classes, must give rise to double words and double ideals.

How true that was even as I sat in the seminar on Twain and *Adventures of Huckleberry Finn.*

As I sat in class, I understood for the fifty-third time what Du Bois really meant. I, too, had a double consciousness. I lived a double life. Every time I gathered for class, I was on edge, defensive, and protective of being called "nigger" by whites—including Twain and Huck Finn. But as soon as I went home or to church or to the historically Black university or another gathering of all Blacks, the word *nigger* or its hybrid *nigga* was back in use. In a different way. Or was it? One day, as I walked into the hallway of the church, Brother Calvin Logan, who is elderly, said to me, "Man, did you see that bunch of niggas on the corner of Idlewood Avenue and Meadow Street? About ten or twelve of 'em?"

"Hey man, you know, I don't quite understand it. Cold as it is. Just standing there ogling and talking trash most of the day," I said.

"Them niggas need to get a job."

"Come on now. Don't be so hard on your own people. You a nigger too, you know. And so am I."

"I know dat. I ain't hard on 'em. I'm jus' saying, they need to go to work somewhere and get off the street corner shucking and jiving. What's wrong with getting a job? A J.O.B.," he asked.

"Nothing is wrong with it. I just don't think it's as simple as that. Maybe they can't find a job."

"Oh, yes it is. It's that simple. There are jobs out there."

"Maybe they can't find a decent job, one that will get them out of poverty," I said.

"Oh, so now it got to be a *decent* job, huh? I'm saying any job is better than cussing, stealing, smoking, and standing idle on the corner."

"I see what you mean. But, suppose they never finished high school?"

"It's good to finish school and go to college even. But . . . some of them niggas don't want to work. That's what I think." "No-o. You can't say that. Most people want to work. Honestly. Black people have always been hard workers. From slavery 'til now." I was adamant about that.

So the use of the hybrid *nigga* by Blacks is a part of the double consciousness and the double standard in Black linguistics, I thought to myself. But, for now, let's continue with Mark Twain and his use of the forbidden word.

The use of the vile and white supremacist racial epithet *nigger* is what makes Mark Twain's novel *Adventures of Huckleberry Finn* an American classic. It started out as the "veriest trash" for whites and now it is almost universally acclaimed as an American classic. The truth is the word *nigger* is always derogatory towards Blacks and Twain did not use the word to describe anyone else in the book except Blacks. Its use is ultimately racial. But this is not what white society objected to in Twain. They were pretty much of one mind concerning the word. It was the satirizing of white religion, aristocracy, etc. that caused such a stir. In March 1885, the *Boston Evening Transcript* newspaper reported that *Huckleberry Finn* was excluded from the library by the Concord (Massachusetts) Public Library committee. The committee pondered the book's immorality, humor, coarseness, and inelegance. One member of the committee regarded the book as "veriest trash." Likewise, the Springfield *Republican*, in March 1885, responded in agreement with the Concord Public Library's banning of *Huckleberry Finn* as "trashy and vicious." I wonder why. No, I know why.

Also in a letter to the Omaha *World-Herald*, August 23, 1902, a citizen wrote that

Huck Finn's new adventure . . . is doing much harm. It has started a number of hitherto spotless people to reading *Adventures of*

Huckleberry Finn, out of natural human curiosity to learn what
this is all about—people who had not heard of him before, people
whose morals will go to rack and ruin now.

Well, let me tell you something. I reasoned that for whites
the novel is trash because of their perception of the way they
were being portrayed by Twain—as murderers, liars, racists,
duplicitous religious hypocrites, and the like. However, years
later, to Blacks like John Wallace, the NAACP, and the Urban
League, the chief objection was to the ubiquitous use of the
racial epithet *nigger*, and to saying the word in mixed-race
public school classrooms where the opportunity for miseducation and misinterpretation is as prevalent as the opportunity to advance the learning process. Maybe even more so. It
depends on the qualifications of the teacher.

The mistreatment of Blacks embedded in the laws and cus-
toms of American democracy and in the construction of capitalist and colonialist theory and practices helps to define and
describe the nature and meaning of the United States of America. From slavery to Jim Crowism to today, the word *nigger* in
the mouths of whites is never positive but represents the meaning of the hated Other. Blacks. African Americans. Former
slaves.

Twain's use of *nigger* seems to flow from his pen with a fre-
quency unsurpassed by any other adjective or noun in the text.
Because the word was so embedded in the psyche of America it
seems to move beyond irony to a level that suggests that Twain,
like his readers, used the word without forethought. Twain's use
of the word *nigger* so often suggests to me a natural use—one
that is so much a part of his being white that he does not
have to think twice about its use. The fact that the slave Jim,
a thirty-something-year-old Black man with a family, is considered inferior to Huck, a thirteen- or fourteen-year-old

white boy of questionable moral character and low social class, was ingrained into the cultural self-perception of Huck and Jim. The colonized take on the attributes and character of the inferior and oppressed other as defined by the oppressor or the colonizer. Niggers are created or made by white folks. It is a racial and social construction.

American chattel slavery was the most dehumanizing form of colonization practiced during the era. It was based on economic exploitation and the belief that Blacks were inhuman. It was a project of creating the hated Other, grounded in an understanding that redefined the nature of being human. Frantz Fanon says that "it is the racist who creates his inferior."

Enslaved Blacks had their lack of human status constitutionalized by the *Dred Scott* decision of 1857; they had the three-fifths clause affirmed and enforced by US Supreme Court in *Plessy v. Ferguson*. It was easy for Twain and Huckleberry Finn to model the existing cultural practices of white supremacy. Fanon reiterates, "Once and for all I will state this principle. A given society is racist or it is not."

Because *Adventures of Huckleberry Finn* is set in a racist location during a time when colonialist ideology was entrenched in the structure of American democracy, the word *nigger* could be used with such ease. And nobody uses the word with the same ease as Mark Twain. The casual use of the racial epithet by Twain forces me and a few others to believe that he and his protagonist, Huck, were only as racist as the next white person of their time periods. They were products of colonialism and endowed with a type of white supremacy that accompanied their racial status. To be white in America means privilege. Legacy status. This does not mean that Twain was necessarily unsympathetic toward the cause of Black freedom, nor does it mean that he was not troubled or torn by his own privileged status as a white man. However, it does mean that he could not rid himself of

the colonialist culture of which he was a product and a beneficiary. Twain's own selfhood was caught up in the dialectic of
good and evil, right and wrong, culture critic and beneficiary
of colonialist and capitalistic practices. Hear me out, now.
I think that he was ambivalent toward Blacks and whites. It
seems that Twain had to keep one foot in both worlds. This put
him in a position of straddling the fence—caught in the middle. This dilemma accounts for his use of the racial epithet *nigger*, his apparent love of Jim, and yet his acts of evil against Jim,
which are evidenced by Huck's not-so-compassionate tricks.

Clearly, I think that Twain expresses this ambiguity through
his protagonist Huck, who vacillates between truth and lie, good
and bad, serious friend and taunting prankster. In one example,
when Huck is thinking about turning on Jim, Huck says,

> I was paddling off, all in a sweat to tell on him; but when he says this
> it seemed to kind of take the tuck all out of me. When I was fifty
> yards off, Jim says: Dah you goes, de ole true Huck; de on'y white
> genlman dat ever kep' his promise to ole Jim. Well, I just felt sick.

And, later in the same chapter, Huck continues expressing his
feelings:

> I got aboard the raft, feeling bad and low, because I knowed very
> well I had done wrong. . . . Then I thought a minute, and says
> to myself, hold on,—s'pose you'd a done right and give Jim up;
> would you felt better than what you do now? No, say I, I'd feel
> bad—I'd feel just the same way I do now. . . . I was stuck.

This being stuck, as Huck says, is indicative of the similar position that Twain found himself in—stuck between a culture and
society grounded in colonialist ideology and practice and his
belief that there was something "awful" wrong with this culture

and his status in it. This notion of being stuck suggests that Twain himself is in a perpetual ethical dilemma that impinges on his self-understanding and his main character with a tension and pressure that makes one feel "awful" bad at times.

I still love the novel as much as the next person. But I'm torn because I love and hate the novel and Mark Twain for being so slippery and so very clever. I have a dialectical relationship with the writer and the novel. Fact and fiction. Love and hate. Admiration and disgust.

Dr. John Wallace, a Chicago educator, has led the public crusade against the use of the book, arguing that the frequent references to "nigger" and Twain's use of rural Black dialect are both demeaning and insulting to Blacks. Most people don't buy that. Personally, I think the dialect is close to perfect.

Lenny Kleinfield, a drama critic, and Jack Saltzman, an American literature professor, argue that Mark Twain is using irony to expose how the minds of white people have been poisoned toward Blacks. Saltzman says, "The problem erupts because readers fail to understand why a writer would use a term like 'nigger Jim' to expose racism." Saltzman locates the problem in the failure of the reader rather than in the failure of the writer or the text itself. And contrary to Stephen L. Carter's recent assertion in *Time* magazine (Summer 2008) that Twain does not refer to Jim as "nigger Jim," I maintain that Twain clearly does say "nigger Jim." And he says it in more than one way. And, even if he doesn't say "nigger Jim," he says "nigger" way too much.

Mr. Meshach Taylor, the actor who played the role of the slave Jim in the dramatic version of *Huckleberry Finn* at the Goodman Theater in Chicago, read the book and felt that it was "one of the best indictments against racism . . . I had ever read."

On the other hand, John Wallace says that "the book is certainly the most racist book, among many, that is printed in the United States of America."

He repeatedly labels it "racist trash." I would never go that far. Never would I say such a thing. Racist, yes; trash, no. Ted Koppel questioned the necessity of banning the entire book but says,

> If I had a child in a school, and I was Black and the child was required to read from that book and repeat the word "nigger" several times, I can see how that would be painful, how that would be offensive.

Damn right. Nat Hentoff, a novelist and syndicated columnist, joins the panel and essentially suggests that the use of the novel in junior high and high school is OK because it demystifies language by its use of the term *nigger*. He says that John Wallace unwittingly underestimates the intelligence and learning ability of Black kids by trying to ban the teaching of the book. Everybody agrees that not every English literature teacher is qualified to teach such a novel to youth. It's too complicated. Too emotional. I understand the debate because I'm in my sixties now and the word *nigger* throughout the novel troubles me mightily.

In *The Fire Next Time*, James Baldwin says, "You can only be destroyed by believing that you really are what the white world calls a *nigger*. I tell you this because I love you, and please don't you ever forget it."

Well, maybe Baldwin was right. Maybe not. Belief has nothing to do with it. No Black person believes that he is a nigger. Not if she or he has read one page of American history. And, even if you can't read, when you hear whites use the word, you know in your spirit that it is intended to harm. It is racist.

Western literature and art are represented by words Mark Twain places in the mouths of his characters, especially Huck, and by the minstrelsy and stereotypical depiction of Blacks by

Twain's illustrator, E. W. Kimble. There is a persistent racial and cultural hierarchy that permeates the written and visual texts of *Adventures of Huckleberry Finn*. This does mean that Twain was a racist, and he certainly took advantage of being white.

Postcolonialism involves remembering and recovering the meanings of past life situations. Homi Bhabha says,

> Memory is the necessary and sometimes hazardous bridge between colonialism and the question of cultural identity. Remembering . . . is never a quiet act of introspection or retrospection. It is a painful remembering, a putting together of the dismembered past to make sense of the trauma of the present.

This is why we should never forget the nature of America's past, particularly as it relates to the treatment of Native Americans and African Americans. Especially those whom America has historically labeled "niggers."

The voyage to America, the Middle Passage, the haunting journey to hell was itself traumatic, and then to be auctioned to the likes of George Washington and Thomas Jefferson, the duplicitous defenders of individual liberty and justice for all, is a contrast that must forever be made to loom large in the consciousness of all Americans. For example, it is believed among Black folk in Virginia that Thomas Jefferson, unlike George Washington, traded his slaves. This made him a much more callous and vulgar capitalist than those slave owners such as Washington who sought to be more humane within a very inhumane culture of slavery. This is probably a distinction without a difference. There was no such thing as a happy slave. Propaganda *be* damned. The language of slavery and humanity is a true dialectic, an oxymoron. Slavery was bestial and savage. Indeed, the past is prologue, as my son Corey says, or as William Faulkner asserts, "The past is never past" when it comes

to American chattel slavery. It is present in the colonialist conscience of those who continue to oppress and discriminate
against people of any color. And it is present in the memories
and the painful reality of African Americans who are able to
sense injustice intuitively and instinctively, and even today can
still feel the pain of the lynchings and the lashings of those
called "niggers" who were caught trying to escape to freedom
or just trying to live as human beings. I can smell racism and
injustice and evil. Sifting and sniffing it out like a hound dog.
We have seen it in the recent murders of Black people—shot in
the back by white racist police or strangled to death by the knee
of Derek Chauvin on the neck of George Floyd. Nine minutes
and twenty-nine seconds. That's the real manifestation of being
treated in a way that signifies the meaning of Twain's ubiquitous "nigger."

Chapter 16

German and Jewish writers use Auschwitz as the measuring rod of human suffering. As an African American, the Atlantic slave trade and the economics of violence, alongside the slave auction block and the extirpation of one's native language, are terrible facts of history and violence. Jacques Derrida's dictum in *Monolingualism of the Other*, "I only have the one language and that language is not mine," describes the condition of African Americans in the United States who are the most blatant examples of the "excluded" as well as the "Other."

This is also evident in Mark Twain's *Adventures of Huckleberry Finn*, where we see "niggers" are excluded from the human race/species:

"Good gracious! Anybody hurt?"
   "No'm. Killed a nigger."
   "Well, it's lucky; because sometimes people do get hurt."

These words by Aunt Sally reflect the cultural mindset of white supremacy and the pandemic absence of any connection between Americanism and concern for Black personhood. African Americans, like the Jews must never forget the Holocaust, must never forget the slavery, the bondage, and the colonialist culture represented by the words of Aunt Sally in the novel. Twain made sure of that. And, yet, most readers seem to brush this aside as simply literary genius. It is genius, but is that all it is? No, it is racism and white supremacy.

My mind vectors toward a feeling of anger and befuddlement every time I read the word *nigger* in Twain's *Adventures of Huckleberry Finn*. When I was in high school, in Chester, Virginia, during the late 1960s, this book was not on the reading list and, like Huck, "I's mighty glad it warn't." For me, the reading of *Huckleberry Finn* vis-à-vis the visual text remains a very difficult task even at my age. I find no humor in the vastly exaggerated images of the Black body throughout the novel. As a humorist, Twain is not funny to me. This is the irony. Likewise the cover of the *New Yorker* magazine where Barack and Michelle Obama were portrayed in combat boots, an afro hairdo, a turban, Osama Bin Laden's half picture, and a flag burning in the fireplace also escapes the imagination of African Americans who do not find the cover funny. Black folk do understand irony and satire better than Twain does. This is what the Black public intellectual Cornel West calls *niggerization*. And for many whites, it is not absurd. It reinforces what they already believe. It is equivalent to Twain's nigger in *Huckleberry Finn*. Satire works too well for Black people. It reinforces the stereotype that it was intended to obviate. Satire does not do Barack Obama any favors in the eyes of those who already believe that he is a Muslim and a threat to the sanctity of the White House or that he was not born in America. What's wrong with being a Black Muslim anyway? Remember Muhammad Ali and Malcolm X. Two American icons. Oh, forgive me. I forgot they are what some call "niggers," too. I say again and again that the art by E. W. Kemble is as demeaning as the use of the racial epithet *nigger* on almost every page of Twain's book. The art speaks its own language. The same language as the forbidden word. Just like the art on the cover of the *New Yorker*. This is the way I feel about it. Again, Stephen L. Carter suggests that it makes no sense in the twenty-first century to ask if Twain was a racist. You be the judge. White privilege and white supremacy are at least first cousins, if not brothers and sisters. They are the two sides of racism.

It is pretty clear that Twain is spoofing white culture and its false sense of superiority through many of the novel's characters, but the word *nigger* throughout the novel seems to have more than tropic use. In other words, is *nigger* a figure of speech or is it more than figurative and more than speech? Twain does provide us with a metalanguage in his use of the racial epithet *nigger*. So how is he using the term in the text even if it is a trope or figure of speech? The use of the term is indicative of the extent to which Twain himself was a part of this colonialist culture, such that he, as a white man of privilege, had internalized the language of colonization in a casual, matter-of-fact way. The banality of the word *nigger* in the book and in the culture is what troubles me so. It would be different if Twain used the word *nigger*, let's say, only one hundred times. That's pretty ubiquitous and endemic. But no, he uses it more than two hundred and eleven times. This fusion of his own colonialist culture and his literary skill help to confound his metalinguistic use of the term *nigger*. Satire can be used to obfuscate the writer's own biases and prejudices. The author's own feelings and beliefs can be shielded by the mask of the literary device. At a minimum, and by any standard, Mark Twain's use of the racial epithet *nigger* is over the top.

Again, ironically, my experience of Twain's use of the racial epithet *nigger* makes *Adventures of Huckleberry Finn* a true American classic. Whether satire, irony, or metaphor, the word *nigger* is an American literary trope that Twain uses so effectively that *Adventures of Huckleberry Finn* will, as far as I can imagine, remain an American classic. This word, this racial slur, this bigoted epithet in the minds and mouths of whites is a true Americanism.

Twain's use of the forbidden word *nigger* went on and on. . . . It never ended, and it *never* lost its power to hurt me.

What about Blacks' use of the word for public consumption? On the airways in hip-hop and rap music? How do I feel when

Blacks claim they have flipped the word? Can the word be totally flipped? Whenever I complain about the lyrics of rap music to my teenage sons, they push my concern aside. They dismiss me as "too serious." My oldest son, Corey, was a precocious child. I remember during his second or third birthday party, I picked up another little boy and held him up in my arms to welcome him to the party and Corey yelled, "Drop him, Daddy" and began pulling at my legs in a jealous rage. I had to put the little boy down because of the protest. My son was upset by my action, but he soon grew out of this type of jealous behavior.

His language and attitude became much more nuanced as he grew older. I remember I used to tell him to always look out for his younger brother, Cameron, another precocious child.

"Corey, watch Cam and make sure he doesn't get hurt."

"Dad, he is as big as I am. He can take care of himself."

"No, he can't. You are his older brother. He is your responsibility," I would say. I think Corey hated this. It was a burden that he did not ask for. But I wanted them both to grow up protecting one another. Corey always felt that he got the short end of the stick because he was the oldest. I always felt Cameron looked up to his older brother and when Corey went off to college, Cameron was very lonesome and sad. I could see it in his eyes. In his behavior. He never said anything, but he internalized the absence. His big brother that he often antagonized had gone off to college and, in a sense, he felt abandoned. He had had a good example in his older brother. Someone he could respect and emulate. What no one knows is that I felt abandoned too. As each of them went off to college, I felt both happy and sad. I'm sure I was more lonely than they were because my whole life up to that point was devoted to their wants and needs.

Corey always felt that Cameron was spoiled: that he was favored because he didn't have to do certain things like put out the trash, cut the grass, or clean his room on a regular basis.

"Dad, you are spoiling the boy. He doesn't even put out the trash."

"You know he's afraid of dogs. Remember the last time he went out near dusk and the neighbor's big wolf-like dog frightened him?"

"Dad, that makes no sense. He's been spoiled by you and Mom."

"Yes, Corey, You're probably right. I'm just doing the best I know how. I don't know everything."

Cameron excelled in elementary school beyond the achievement of his brother. But as he grew older, he, like his brother, was resistant to high academic standards and achievement. It took all of my energy to make sure that both of them would stay in school and excel, and not be influenced by those who were in school for reasons other than getting a good education. This applied to teachers and students. Keeping our boys in school through college was a very difficult challenge, but we felt compelled to do it. We wanted to give them every opportunity to achieve in the midst of indifference by self, teachers, and peers. From time to time, they felt that academic excellence was "whack." That it was not cool to be a scholar. This is so prevalent in Black culture. My greatest challenge as a father was to make sure that my sons were focused on the future and not too preoccupied with immediate gratification. I wanted them to set some goals and strive toward achieving those goals one day at a time. One grade level at a time. These were the greatest days of my life. The most rewarding times of my life. I miss their childhood much more than they do. Some days, I sit in silence and wish that those days could return. But like time itself when it's gone, it is gone in every way except in the deep recesses of memory.

In retrospect, I feel I could have done more to prepare them for the challenges of a cold and callous world. I keep second-guessing myself. "Maybe we should have never sent them to public schools," I say to myself. "Maybe they should have been home-schooled. Maybe more private lessons in writing, poetry, music, and mathematics. Maybe this. Maybe that." I don't really know the answer to these never-ending doubts. These haunting questions of second-guessing engulf me as I learn more and more about their struggles. I was so busy focusing on the big picture of racism and injustice that I failed to concentrate on their particular development. Of course they fought me on every hand. Parenting is 50 percent guesswork coupled with 50 percent faith and prayer. Nobody really knows what he's doing. Even Abraham, the father of the faith, in the book of Genesis, almost murdered his own son. Thank God for the ram in the bush.

My son used to say about the use of "nigga" or profanity in rap songs: "Dad, it don't mean nothing."

"How could it not mean something?" I said.

"Because it's just music, that's all."

"You mean to tell me that it has no effect on the way you think about yourself and others? That's unbelievable," I said.

"Dad, you're making too much out of this."

"I don't think so, Corey. This has to do with the whole history of a people. This has to do with slavery, racism, self-esteem, and Black consciousness."

"I don't know, Dad. It's not that serious."

"Right. You don't know and neither do I. But I know that no other group uses vile racist epithets to describe themselves in the public arena. I think this is Black capitalist exploitation of its own people. Self-hatred." Greed.

"Dad, you're too race conscious. You don't understand."

"Maybe that's the issue. I'm trying to understand myself and others. And, I don't get it. I'm conflicted and I'm confused. How Black rappers can put the forbidden word in the lyrics to every song to be played all over the world. Do they know the history and pain of this word? People were hanged. Lynched. Beaten and flogged."

"Dad, it's just music. It don't mean nothing."

"It does mean something. The beat means something, the words mean something: Niggers. Bitches. Hos. Baby mommas," I said.

One of my graduate students recently told me about his travels to Brazil and South Africa. He related how the word *nigger* has found its way into cultures that know nothing of Black suffering in America epitomized by the use of the word *nigger*. Niggers were slaves. Niggers were lynched. Niggers were spat on. Niggers were hanged. Electrocuted. Sold on the auction block. Branded like cattle. I repeat all this so that we don't ever forget.

"What happened?" I asked the student. "Tell me about your experience," I said.

"As I arrived in Rio de Janeiro, a little boy of twelve was selling his wares—necklaces, bracelets, and things," he explained.

"Yeah, OK. I get the picture."

"The little fair-skinned boy came up to me and said in broken English, 'Nigger, I give you good deal on this bracelet. Five dollars, for you, nigger. Just five American dollars.'"

"I was stunned and speechless at being called a 'nigger' halfway across the world," he said.

I said, "That's the international and global impact of rap and hip-hop music."

It is because people around the world hear Black folk calling themselves and each other niggers on CDs and videos that they feel that they too can call a Black person a "nigger." They hear it, so they say it. All Blacks are now niggers in Johannesburg, Tokyo, San Jose; in Ghana, Kenya, Bangalore, Beijing, and Sarajevo. You name the places where rap and hip-hop are played and you will hear the word *nigger* coming from the "mouths of babes and infants," just like it was when Mark Twain wrote *Adventures of Huckleberry Finn* in 1886.

Chapter 17

It is springtime now. I can feel the afternoon heat and smell the fragrance of the flowers as we sit in class. It's the last day of class and I have a lot to think about. The tension in me is still palpable and the day promises a lot of drama because the course stirred up a lot of my past and emotions that caused me to search my own soul and to look more deeply at myself. I still don't understand certain things. My struggles continue as I pretend to have my feelings under control. And, so I keep struggling to balance this failure in my soul with a hope that I can succeed in changing my own feeble and confused mind.

It is no secret. Black folk have historically referred to themselves as "niggas" in imitation of the colonizers. Yes, that's what I call it, imitating. Jim, the "nigger" slave in Mark Twain's American classic refers to other Black slaves as "niggers," adopting the same language as Huck Finn, Miss Watson, Tom Sawyer, and others in the dominant culture. Jim says, "Dey's mighty good to me, dese niggers is . . ." The use of *nigger* to refer to the self and other Blacks reflects the negative impact of oppression and white supremacy upon Black identity and culture. The commercial use of the variant *nigga* by Black rappers and writers is as American as capitalism itself. Almost every Black rapper today uses the word *nigga* as ubiquitously as Mark Twain used the racially bigoted epithet *nigger*. What's the difference? Well, some say it depends on who is talking. When Blacks use the term in private among friends, its meaning is thought to be crystal clear and does not suffer from the same suspicion that it does when whites use the term. To most, it supposedly suggests comradeship, spiritual connectedness, and familiarity. But to me it is offensive. It still makes me cringe in most instances. The only difference is found in the way I hear the word when used by Blacks among Blacks. I don't hear hatred and vileness, but I still hear *nigger*.

Recently, I was driving from Richmond to Raleigh, North Carolina, and got lost looking for the particular church I was trying to find. I was scheduled to speak there for a conference on the Unity and Togetherness of Black males.

Lost, we pulled off Highway 98 East to ask for directions. It was a Chubby's gas station near a Martin Luther King Boulevard somewhere between Raleigh and Durham. There was a young Black lady behind the counter.

"Could you tell me how to get to Richardson Avenue? I'm looking for New Canaan Baptist Church," I said.

"I'm not sure I can be much help. I'm not good at locating places, but my husband might be able to help you. He's in the blue car right there." She pointed her finger toward the large glass window.

I went outside to the blue car. There was a Black man working on some wires under the dashboard. The front seat was pushed all the way back and he was sprawled on the floor with his back against the seat. I grunted and tried to get his attention.

"Excuse me, sir. Excuse me," I said.

He snapped, "Nigga, what do you want?" with his hands still fumbling under the dashboard.

"Your wife told me to ask you how I could get from here to Richardson Avenue," I said.

"Nigga, I ain't got time to be fooling with you about no directions. I gotta fix my AC." He barely looked up from what he was doing, but I could see the gold fronts in his mouth as he spoke with absolute annoyance and disinterest.

He didn't look me in the face nor did he stop doing what he was doing. He could see my black hands and arms. That's all. Yet, he referred to me as "nigga." I was not really shocked or angered by this. Yet I was not about to debate this total stranger about the Black-on-Black use of the forbidden word. Today the word is forbidden by everyone except Blacks. That's what troubled me the most. I did not know this man and he did not know me. Yet he called me nigga. Here I was dressed in a designer suit and tie, on my way to a conference to address Black males about self-esteem and empowerment, being addressed without forethought as "nigga" by a Black male who had internalized his own oppression. He saw himself and all Blacks as niggas. At that very moment, the offensive, vile nature of the word and its hybridized form became even more evident to me.

Not all Blacks are in agreement on this. Ask Cornel West or Michael Eric Dyson. Ask Randall Kennedy. Ask Ludacris. Ask Oprah Winfrey or Terrence Howard. Ask Whoopi Goldberg. Rappers and hip-hop artists seem to use the term as a way to sell records, in the same way that Mark Twain used the word *nigger* to sell books. This is the lure of vulgar capitalism. I believe that the same reasoning applies to rappers and comics now as applied to Twain back then. The flippers have been flipped. Richard Pryor, the late Black comic, won a Grammy award when he began to use the word *nigga* in every other line of his comedy routine. I don't have to tell you that Blacks are often rewarded for self-denigration and racial diminution of the pride that otherwise keeps Blacks thinking and acting on a higher plane.

It is clear that almost anything negative in which Blacks participate is rewarded in American culture. Denzel Washington and Halle Berry won Oscars for best actor/actress for movies that reflect Black stereotypes and negative archetypes—drugs, hustling, corruption, and hyper-sexuality. Black-on-Black crime is a perfect example of this social reality. When Blacks murder each other, or when they are murdered by whites, there is less chance of receiving the death penalty or a long prison term. The reward for ridding society of "niggers" is subtle but quite clear. Blacks and whites know that the penalties are different—that justice in the courts is not color blind. It never was and it never will be as long as the "color line," as W. E. B. Du Bois terms it, remains a central problem in American culture. The word *nigga* in the mouths of Black rappers sells records. It's that simple. It's that complicated. There is a market for the negative or the glamorized version of self-destruction—the version denuded of its authentic history.

The gangsta rap group Three Six Mafia won an Oscar for best song in a motion picture. The song, "It's Hard out Here for a Pimp," reflects a negative element in Black culture and suggests that pimping is normal among Blacks. Stereotypes. Negativity. This language also suggests that Black women are commodities and the sale of the Black body is something that Black vulgar capitalists learned from the slave masters. Think about it for a minute. Unfortunately, the music and entertainment moguls have rewarded this negativity in an effort to cast Black culture as deviant and morally feckless. I mean weak and evil. I do not want to take anything from Three Six Mafia or any musical group, but it is important to realize that negative images and language about Blacks is a form of self-hatred and the internalization of hundreds of years of oppression and slavery. Also, it is criminal to mistreat Black women, who represent the best of Black culture. That's what the slave master did. What's the difference? Rappers and poets, please tell me so that I can understand myself and others more fully. So that I can understand you.

The song "It's Hard out Here for a Pimp" suggests that Blacks have not fully mastered the art and practice of raising capital and making a profit at the expense of dehumanizing others. The pimp trope in the song and in the broader culture is symbolized by greed, physical violence, women as sex objects, egoism, sexual exploitation, and vulgar capitalism. To suggest that pimping is hard is to equate it with decent, honest work, which it is not. Professional sports figures are also pimped as they are traded from one team to another for money. This means that they are bid on much like slaves were as they were placed on the auction block. Look at the words to the pimp song by the gangsta rap singers and composers Three Six Mafia:

> You know it's hard out here for a pimp (you ain't knowin). . . . Because a whole lot of bitches talkin shit (you ain't knowin). . . . [Chorus] Niggaz hatin on me cause I got, hoes on the tray. . . . North Memphis where I'm from, I'm 7th Street bound, Where niggaz all the time end up lost and never found.

I don't understand. I don't understand this at all. Some of my young Black male students have suggested to me that whites are fearful of young urban Blacks. While this may be the case on an individual, subjective scale, it is a general fallacy and untruth. Remember slavery. Bull Connor. Montgomery. Rodney King. The Jena Six. And recently, Trayvon Martin's murder in a gated community in Sanford, Florida. And the deaths of George Floyd and Breonna Taylor . . . Blacks do not harm white folk as a general rule, but the reverse is not true. Blacks have historically been victims of white violence, symbolized by lynchings and police murdering Blacks for sport. My response is to ask where is the historical data to support such a thesis? And on what basis does one make such an argument? Their responses are usually anecdotal and sometimes wishful thinking. Fiction. I remind them that white folks held Blacks in bondage, in chattel slavery for nearly two hundred and fifty years in the United States, and for some of that time, Black slaves outnumbered whites by two to one, five to one, and ten to one. This same principle was true in South Africa and in other colonized countries where the natives often outnumbered the colonizers by as much as one hundred or a thousand to one. How does this translate into white fear? Please explain that to me. How can one white man hold a hundred Black men and women in subjugation? What makes for such domination? It seems to me that the logic has been misconstrued. It would be more logical to assert that Blacks are really afraid of white people! Otherwise, there would be more Nat Turners, Gabriel Prossers, or Denmark Veseys in the annals our history. Now, is that reasonable or what? Think, my brothers and sisters. Use your God-given brains. Or is it true that Black people love white people? Explain that to me, da blame it.

The word *nigger*, a concept of race in American history and culture, is an imaginative construction by whites whose nature and purpose was to dominate the Other. In this sense, race is as much a fictive enterprise as American democracy's assertion that "all men are created equal" and that "life, liberty, and the pursuit of happiness" was the expressed purpose of the founding fathers. Pure fiction. This language never included the ultimate excluded Other—the Black slave, the so-called nigger.

Africans left the shores of West Central Africa as human beings—sons and daughters of priests and kings, tribal chiefs, and leaders—and arrived at Jamestown, Richmond, and Norfolk as chattel slaves. They were property like dogs and cattle. Like cotton and tobacco. Even their native languages were forced out of them. Intentionally. Hatefully and with malice. They left behind ancient civilizations and notable empires and arrived in America with a determination to hold on to their distinctive folklore, languages, music, foods, religion, artifacts, crafts, and rituals. Their being was reduced to the status of saleable property. The Middle Passage, however, required strength of mind and body and determination and desire to survive against all odds. Those who survived the tumultuous seas and the dehumanizing conditions of being treated like hogs and dogs had to face the plantation owners and the American economic system of exploitation and greed, symbolized most vividly by the slave auction block and nearly three centuries of wageless labor. The so-called nigger built America with his/her blood, sweat, and muscles. Tears too.

Just as the nigger is a creation of white supremacy, the white man is also a creation of his own imagination. He is no more white and superior than the Black person is a nigger. This is where the imbrication of fiction and nonfiction becomes fused. There are indeed elements of fiction in nonfiction, and there are elements of nonfiction in fiction. Ask any writer who is willing to tell the truth and you'll find that his or her truth is often encumbered by fiction. This is seen vividly regarding the issue of racial identity. It is an accepted truth that white slave owners took sexual liberties with their slaves, both male and female. The slave master was complicit with the laws and courts in the general American understanding that slaves were inhuman, from a theological, constitutional, cultural, religious, and sociopolitical perspective. Yet the master regularly copulated with the young beautiful Black females, creating a mixed race of individuals who are as white genetically as they are Black. This is the ugly truth about America that certain Democrats and Republicans continue to brush aside. I submit Thomas Jefferson as exhibit A. According to both law and custom, the offspring of this miscegenated cohabitation was Black, a mulatto—a nigger like Helga Crane in Nella Larsen's novel *Passing*. The forbidden word *nigger*, like chattel slavery, free labor, and vulgar capitalism, is a recurring trope in the American story—a story where fact and fiction have joined hands in unholy matrimony and revisionist history glosses over facts and truth. Listen to the dialogue in Dick Gregory's autobiography:

> The police stopped us after one block and told us we couldn't parade through the city. . . . It was a Greenwood policeman.
>
> "Move on, nigger."
>
> "Thanks a million."
>
> "Thanks for what?"
>
> "Up North police don't escort me across the street against a red light."
>
> "I said, move on, nigger."
>
> "I don't know my way. I'm new in this town. . . . Ask that white woman over there to come here and show me where to go."
>
> The cop's face got red, and there was spittle at the corner of his mouth. All he could say was, "nigger, dirty nigger . . ."
>
> I looked at him. "Your mama's a nigger. Probably got more Negro blood in her than I could ever hope to have in me."
>
> He dropped my other arm then, and backed away, and his hand was on his gun. I thought he was going to explode.

The preceding words quoted from *Nigger: An Autobiography*, by Dick Gregory with Robert Lipsyte, are indicative of the way society uses the word *nigger* as a racial epithet toward Blacks in the United States.

Again, one of the most highly acclaimed American novels is the nineteenth-century classic *Adventures of Huckleberry Finn*. The ubiquitous use of the word *nigger* throughout the novel is evidenced by the more than 220 times this racial epithet is employed by Mark Twain. In spite of the criticism and the efforts by some to ban the reading of the book by high school literature classes, the book has been lauded and applauded by the likes of C. S. Lewis and Toni Morrison. Its language and dialect are also its major strengths. In the preface to the Norton Critical Edition, the editor Thomas Cooley states,

> Mark Twain's greatest achievement in *Huck Finn*, perhaps was to make a spoken language do everything a literary language alone could do before him. Nothing is lost when Huck describes his panic in the fog, or the coming of a storm, or Pap's malice, or Jim's kindness—all in the vocabulary and syntax of the uneducated son of the town drunk, whose special way of seeing beyond conventional prejudices required an unconventional way of speaking.

The unconventional way of speaking does not obviate the conventional white supremacist language inherent in the use of the word *nigger* by Twain. This colonialist use of racial language is demonstrated in Pap's speech about "niggers" and voting. The diatribe against the government shows Mark Twain's ability to use dialect and voice the illogic and racism of the times through Pap, the town drunk and Huck's father.

The notion of the inferiority of the Black person was deeply ingrained in the consciousness and culture of nineteenth-century America, and vestiges of this notion remain. It shows the fictive thinking that racism constructs. Pap's palavering against the government, voting, and niggers is symptomatic of the reality of white supremacy in both Pap, the character, Mark Twain, the writer, and Huck the protagonist. We see this to a lesser extent in other pieces of literature.

Harriett Beecher Stowe's novel *Uncle Tom's Cabin* opens with a conversation between two slave masters—one considered a gentleman, and the other not so gentlemanly in his appearance or his behavior. Notice the conversation while they are discussing the sale of the slave named Tom:

"Why, the fact is, Haley, Tom is an uncommon fellow; he is certainly worth that sum anywhere—steady, honest, capable, manages my whole farm like a clock."

"You mean honest, as niggers go," said Haley, helping himself to a glass of brandy.

"No; I mean, really, Tom is a good, steady, sensible, pious fellow. He got religion at a camp-meeting, four years ago; and I believe he really *did* get it . . ."

"Some folks don't believe there is pious niggers, Shelby," said Haley with a candid flourish of his hand, "but I *do*. . . . Yes, I consider religion a valeyable thing in a nigger, when it's the genuine article, and no mistake."

Mr. Shelby and Haley continue their slave-trading discussion as the five-year-old child of Mr. Shelby's slave Eliza wanders into the room. Eliza, who is nearby, overhears some of the slave-trading conversation between her master and the other trader as they were discussing buying and selling her young son, whom they referred to as Jim Crow:

"I would rather not sell him," said Mr. Shelby, thoughtfully. "The fact is, sir, I'm a humane man, and I hate to take the boy from his mother, sir."

Apparently, some slaveholders were more humane in their inhumanity than others, but the truth is the system was grounded in evil and sustained by indifference, greed, savage violent capitalism, and inhumanity toward Blacks. This is abject delusion that the slave master, Mr. Shelby, possessed. Thinking that he was humane was obviated by the power and force of the economics of American capitalism. The SPCA is more humane than that to its dogs and cats. Where was PETA when Black folk needed them? That same slave master, who said he would hate to separate the boy from his mother, does exactly what he hates to do as he sells Harry and Uncle Tom. Luckily, Eliza is eavesdropping during the discussion between the slave master and his wife by hiding in the closet, and instead of allowing her son Harry to be sold, she decides to run away in the middle of the night. Imagine Eliza as a runaway slave:

> "I'm running away—Uncle Tom and Aunt Chloe—carrying off my child—Master sold him!" "Sold him?" echoed both, lifting up their hands in dismay. "Yes, sold him!" said Eliza, firmly; "I crept into the closet by Mistress' door to-night, and I heard Master tell Missis that he had sold my Harry, and you, Uncle Tom, both, to a trader; and that he was going off this morning on his horse, and that the man was to take possession to-day."

The auction block was one of the most feared and inhumane acts of chattel slavery. The slave auction, either private or public, was a cruel reality. Three hundred dollars. Strong. Child-bearing condition. I often think of this historical fact as Black athletes are auctioned to the highest bidding professional basketball, football, or baseball team's owner. And when they get sick or injured, they too are sold or traded to someone else just as the slaves were. The vestiges of slavery remain and some of its practices are still a part of our culture and economic system. The Black body remains a commodity as the professional and collegiate sports scene vividly demonstrates. Strong legs, hands, and arms. Excellent physical condition. Tall and muscular. Weighs 220 pounds. College degree: not required.

Trading Black slaves, separating mothers, children, husbands, wives, and kindred was one of the most feared and heart-wrenching aspects of American slavery. Eliza, who had no experience in the fields or in negotiating the unknowns of the outdoors, took to the woods, the swamp, and the river to avoid the consequences of her son Harry's sale to the slave trader. Eliza was what they called a "house nigger." It seems to me that not even the fear of death or the consequences of being hunted by bloodhounds and, if caught, being brought back to face the ferocious death of the slave master's whip, could obviate the desire to avoid the auction block or the quest to be free. Freedom at all costs.

The Emancipation Proclamation of 1863 did not end the ravages of unfreedom and racism. Richard Wright, in his collection of novellas, *Uncle Tom's Children*, set in the Deep South during the postslavery era, makes this point perfectly clear. In his autobiographical sketch, *The Ethics of Living Jim Crow*, Wright chronicles his experience with white racism and the word *nigger* in the family's move from Arkansas to Mississippi:

> My first job was with an optical company in Jackson, Mississippi. The morning I applied, I stood straight and neat before the boss, answering all his questions with sharp yes sirs and no sirs . . . that I knew where I was, and that I knew he was a *white* man. . . . He looked me over as though he were examining a prize poodle. . . .
> Boy, how would you like to try to learn something around here? he asked me. "I'd like it fine, sir" I said happy. . . . For the first month I got along ok. Both Peace and Murray seemed to like me. But one thing was missing. And I kept thinking about it. I was not learning anything and nobody was volunteering to help me. Thinking they had forgotten that I was to learn something about the mechanics of grinding lenses I asked Murray one day to tell me about the work. He grew red. "What yuh tryin' t'do, nigger, git smart?" he asked.
> "Naw, I ain't tryin' t' git smart," I said.
> "Well, don't if yuh know what's good for yuh!"
> ". . . this is a *white* man's work around here, and you better watch yourself!"

Richard Wright's next job was as a porter in a clothing store, where he says that his Jim Crow education continued. He observed the boss and his son abuse, drag, and kick a "negro woman" while a white policeman looked on: "'But, that's what we do to niggers when they don't want to pay their bills,' he said, laughing. His son looked at me and grinned."

After working in a hotel in Jackson, Mississippi, Richard Wright moved to Memphis, where his Jim Crow education flourished, and he continued to be called "nigger" and treated with disdain and disrespect. That was then. This is now or is it then?

In the movie *Glory Road*, the story is told of the struggles and ultimate success of a white coach and seven Black basketball players at the mythical Texas Western University in El Paso. The story is set in the heart of the Jim Crow South in 1966, during the days of freedom of choice, which came on the heels of segregation. The story is about determination, white supremacy, injustice, and the ability of a team sport like basketball to advance race pride and uplift. The dialogue in the movie shows how the country moved from using the word *negro* to *Black* to describe a race of people. The term *Black* took on a new pride and meaning in the lexicon of American language usage. I remember when the use of the term *Black* by an African American to describe another African American was cause for a fight: "You Black SOB. You so Black, you make the night look like day." "Don't call me Black. I'll kick your ass. Say it one mo' time and see what happens." This is the effect of colonization, which often leads to brainwashing the colonized such that self-hatred and a desire to emulate the oppressor is internalized. It was only after the term was "flipped" to mean something else that it became a part of the language of the masses and everyone else in the culture. James Brown sang, "Say it loud. I'm Black and I'm proud." And yet, the word Black coupled with *nigger* as in "Black nigger" used to be a double negative even among Black folk. Color is still an issue. Persons of dark complexion have a more difficult time succeeding than lighter-skinned Blacks. This is not always true, but Michael Eric Dyson said recently that it is a part of the reason why he is a distinguished professor who graduated from Princeton University while his brother is in prison. He had more opportunity to succeed because he is light-skinned.

Again, in the 2006 movie *Glory Road*, set in 1965–66, there are several instances where whites used the word *nigger*. On one occasion, as the team is traveling in the heart of the deep South, one of the Black players is ganged up on and brutally beaten while being called "nigger." On another, even more egregious occasion, the hotel room of one player is ransacked and the wall smeared in red paint, to symbolize blood, with the directive "Niggers, go home." The coach in the movie, based on a partially true story, is indeed ahead of his time, but it is clear from the beginning of the film that the coach's interest in Black players developed after none of the white players he tried to recruit were interested in playing for what they perceived to be a second-rate losing team. The movie depicts some of America's enduring issues with race. The issue of race has been the central and abiding dilemma of the American experience.

The recent hoopla by conservative Republicans railing against Critical Race Theory, as if it is not a historical fact that racism is systemic and embedded in law and practice, is simply another manifestation of white supremacy and racism.

Chapter 18

The semester finally came to an end. I had survived a brutal and uncomfortable thirteen weeks of hearing and reading the word *nigger*. Oh, I almost forgot. Remember, the professor had asked each of us to memorize a one-hundred-word passage of the novel and to recite it on the last day. What was I to do? I couldn't bring myself to say the word *nigger* standing in front of an all-white class. I liked so much of the novel, but there was no passage that I wanted to recite that was devoid of the forbidden word *nigger*.

After thirteen long weeks, I still had mixed feelings and my thinking was as cloudy and muddy as the Mississippi River. Ten people had already done their recitation that day. They had no problem. There was no semblance of hesitation by any of them. Again, they were all white. It was now my turn to recite. I was tense. Nervous. My legs felt like they were shackled by iron that weighed a thousand pounds. My knees buckled. My throat was as dry as the Sahara and I was still nervous, but not like I was on the first day of class. A voice welled up in my mind's eye saying, *You can do this. You can do it. Just do it. Go for it.* I could see it on the page. The words were right before my eyes. While I did not have an eidetic memory, these were some words I could never forget. So, I pressed against the table, took a deep breath, and stood up before the class. As every eye zoomed in on me, I began to speak poetic words in defiance of Mark Twain's American classic—words that I had learned as a child by listening to my younger brother Doug recite from Countee Cullen's poem

"Incident." It was reflexive. The words with somber half-muted tension, propped up by rebellion and hope, began to flow slowly from my parched lips:

> *Once riding in old Baltimore,*
> *Heart filled, head-filled with glee;*
> *I saw a Baltimorean*
> *Keep looking straight at me.*
> *Now I was eight and very small,*
> *And he was no whit bigger,*
> *And so I smiled, but he poked out*
> *His tongue, and called me, "Nigger."*
> *I saw the whole of Baltimore*
> *From May until December;*
> *Of all the things that happened there*
> *That's all that I remember.*

And then, before I could sit down, I got a second surge of confidence, and I began to recite from memory's painful past the words of Langston Hughes's poem "Refugee in America":

> *There are words like Freedom*
> *Sweet and wonderful to say.*
> *On my heart-strings freedom sings*
> *All day everyday.*
> *There are words like Liberty*
> *That almost make me cry.*
> *If you had known what I knew*
> *You would know why.*

There was gaping stillness in the room. I had reinterpreted the assignment by asserting my own identity and self-hood. I had redefined American literature by reciting two short poems by Black writers. I could feel the awful, deafening silence. Tears filled my eyes as my heart pounded against my chest. My voice cracked and faded. I plopped down in my seat and folded my face into my hands. I was drained of all my energy. Encountering Twain's use of *nigger* every week on every page for a whole semester had been hard for me—very, very hard. I was teetering on the brink of falling apart, thankful that this was my last assignment. I thought to myself, *I am falling apart.* This was the last day of a class that felt like it had gone on for eternity. It felt like I had been on the battlefield for a thousand years. Luckily, for me and my sanity, the class ended that day as the sun began to fade from the horizon and as I mustered the strength to smile and to experience the empathy other students felt for me. For the first time they seemed to understand my painful struggle and my plight as a Black man in a class that itself was a metaphor, a symbol of the past, present, and postmodern condition of American society. And, for the first time, I tried not to deceive myself and others with stoic poise and the sublimation of my feelings of deep emotional anguish.

I was trembling and my voice was fading into silence as I repeated the last lines of the poem by Langston Hughes: "If you had known what I knew, you would know why."

By then, my knees could barely transport me back to my seat, and my hands, both hands were trembling. I put my hands in my pants pocket and took the five or six long steps back to the chair and plopped my head down on the table and began to breathe a sigh of relief and to say a silent prayer of thanksgiving. I thanked my ancestors Nella Larsen, Zora Neale Hurston, Langston Hughes, Richard Wright, W. E. B. Du Bois, Martin Luther King Jr., Malcolm X, Muhammed Ali, Sojourner Truth, Samuel DeWitt Proctor, Leroy Fowler, Elsie Campbell, Stanley Lucas, and Richard and Carrie Anna Harris for helping me endure and to be strong for this present generation. My standing up and my sitting down meant that I had achieved another educational milestone for my family and me. For my strong and courageous sons, Corey and Cameron, and for my lovely wife, Demetrius. For Black people young and old. I earned the coveted master of arts degree in English literature that very day.

Acknowledgments

Thanks to the many people at writers' workshops and other places who read and offered valuable suggestions and corrections to the entire manuscript or excerpts from it during the past fifteen years: Maureen Baron, Patricia Perry, Richard N. Soulen, Robert Wafawanaka, Jim Meisner Jr., Jerry Gross, Sadia Shepherd, Sidney Offit, Marcel Cornis-Pope, Andrew Blossoms, Susan Hartman, Marita Golden, David Shields, Bruce Jay Friedman, Barbara Clark, Joanne Braxton, Charles Marsh, Yohance Whitaker, and Larry Bouchard.

Thanks to Victor Fisher, associate editor of the Mark Twain Project, and staff of the Bancroft Library at UC Berkeley for facilitating the week I spent scouring their resources and examining some of the Mark Twain Papers in the summer of 2006. These materials have helped broaden my knowledge and understanding of Mark Twain.

Thanks to all of the students in the Mark Twain Seminar and family members who read portions of the manuscript. Paula Watson, Charlotte McSwine, Andrew Blossom, Venessa H. Bond, and my entire staff have read all or portions of this text.

Thanks to the entire Fortress Press leadership and staff—particularly my editor Scott Tunseth and the team at Scribe Inc. for their guidance and support.

Finally, thanks to my sons, James Corey and Cameron C. Harris, and my wife, Demetrius, for their continued love and support.